**New Directions for
Teaching and Learning**

Marilla D. Svinicki
EDITOR-IN-CHIEF

R. Eugene Rice
CONSULTING EDITOR

Curriculum Development in Higher Education:
Faculty-Driven Processes and Practices

Peter Wolf
Julia Christensen Hughes
EDITORS

D1569846

Number 112 • Winter 2007
Jossey-Bass
San Francisco

CURRICULUM DEVELOPMENT IN HIGHER EDUCATION: FACULTY-DRIVEN
PROCESSES AND PRACTICES
Peter Wolf, Julia Christensen Hughes (eds.)
New Directions for Teaching and Learning, no. 112
Marilla D. Svinicki, Editor-in-Chief
R. Eugene Rice, Consulting Editor

Microfilm copies of issues and articles are available in 16mm and 35mm,
as well as microfiche in 105mm, through University Microfilms, Inc.,
300 North Zeeb Road, Ann Arbor, Michigan 48106-1346.

NEW DIRECTIONS FOR TEACHING AND LEARNING (ISSN 0271-0633, electronic ISSN 1536-0768) is part of The Jossey-Bass Higher and Adult
Education Series and is published quarterly by Wiley Subscription Services, Inc., A Wiley Company, at Jossey-Bass, 989 Market Street, San
Francisco, California 94103-1741. Periodicals postage paid at San Francisco, California, and at additional mailing offices. POSTMASTER: Send
address changes to New Directions for Teaching and Learning, Jossey-
Bass, 989 Market Street, San Francisco, California 94103-1741.

New Directions for Teaching and Learning is indexed in CIJE: Current
Index to Journals in Education (ERIC), Contents Pages in Education
(T&F), Current Abstracts (EBSCO), Educational Research Abstracts
Online (T&F), ERIC Database (Education Resources Information Cen-
ter), Higher Education Abstracts (Claremont Graduate University), and
SCOPUS (Elsevier).

SUBSCRIPTIONS cost $85 for individuals and $209 for institutions, agencies,
and libraries in the United States. Prices subject to change. See order form
at end of book.

EDITORIAL CORRESPONDENCE should be sent to the editor-in-chief, Marilla
D. Svinicki, Department of Educational Psychology, University of Texas
at Austin, One University Station, D5800, Austin, TX 78712.

Wiley Bicentennial Logo: Richard J. Pacifico

www.josseybass.com

ISBN: 978-0-470-27851-2

CONTENTS

FROM THE SERIES EDITOR

About This Publication. Since 1980, *New Directions for Teaching and Learning (NDTL)* has brought a unique blend of theory, research, and practice to leaders in postsecondary education. *NDTL* sourcebooks strive not only for solid substance but also for timeliness, compactness, and accessibility.

The series has four goals: to inform readers about current and future directions in teaching and learning in postsecondary education, to illuminate the context that shapes these new directions, to illustrate these new directions through examples from real settings, and to propose ways in which these new directions can be incorporated into still other settings.

This publication reflects the view that teaching deserves respect as a high form of scholarship. We believe that significant scholarship is conducted not only by researchers who report results of empirical investigations but also by practitioners who share disciplines reflections about teaching. Contributors to *NDTL* approach questions of teaching and learning as seriously as they approach substantive questions in their own disciplines, and they deal not only with pedagogical issues but also with the intellectual and social context in which these issues arise. Authors deal on the one hand with theory and research and on the other with practice, and they translate from research and theory to practice and back again.

About This Volume. This issue brings two new perspectives to the series. The first is a more international perspective from the very active and thriving faculty development work being done in Canada. The second topic is curriculum design, something we haven't had as a focus for a while. The authors attempt to blend the very real need for institutions to engage in regular curriculum practice as a growth experience and the important role that faculty can play in that process. In addition, they propose the idea of a scholarship of curriculum practice to complement the scholarship of teaching and learning. They pose the interesting challenge: Shouldn't everything we do in the academy be done in a scholarly manner?

Marilla D. Svinicki
Editor-in-Chief

MARILLA D. SVINICKI is director of the Center for Teaching Effectiveness at the University of Texas at Austin.

EDITORS' NOTES

Faculty in institutions of higher education and their various program committees are increasingly initiating—and in some cases being mandated to engage in—processes of curriculum assessment and reform. Interest is being driven by government and accrediting agency–based quality assurance initiatives, growing attention to student skill and values development, and an increased commitment to supporting these outcomes through learning-centered curricula and constructivist pedagogies. Behind much of this interest is a growing awareness by faculty, employers, governments, and society at large of the important role graduates play in contributing to the knowledge economy and the quality of society, along with the need to equip them with the skills and values that will help them apply and extend disciplinary knowledge in meaningful ways.

This volume focuses on the frameworks used, along with lessons learned, in a variety of curriculum assessment and development processes at the program, departmental, interdisciplinary, faculty, institutional, and provincial levels in higher education. Increasingly faculty are being asked to play leadership roles in initiating and implementing these processes. It is essential that faculty are well prepared for this work and have access to useful frameworks as well as having the opportunity to benefit from the experiences of others. Our hope is that this volume will serve these purposes.

Chapter One, by Harry Hubball and Neil Gold, opens the volume by presenting the broad context for curriculum reform. It provides a brief overview of government-initiated quality assurance initiatives as one catalyst for curricular development. It also argues that curriculum development—in both its processes and its intended outcomes—is also motivated by a commitment to providing students with learning-centered curricula supported by constructivist pedagogical approaches. The chapter's greatest contribution may be its advocacy for a scholarly approach to curriculum development, implementation, and evaluation. Drawing parallels with the scholarship of teaching and learning (SoTL) movement, the authors introduce the concept of the scholarship of curriculum practice (SoCP), which is defined as "an approach to higher education programming that integrates curriculum and pedagogical research in the disciplinary context of a field of study" and additionally includes dissemination and peer review as critical components. For SoCP to flourish, significant institutional support is required.

Chapter Two, by Peter Wolf, explores the processes that have been developed and refined at one teaching development center in support of faculty-driven curricular assessment and development initiatives. The chapter also

NEW DIRECTIONS FOR TEACHING AND LEARNING, no. 112, Winter 2007   © Wiley Periodicals, Inc.
Published online in Wiley InterScience (www.interscience.wiley.com) • DOI: 10.1002/tl.292

1

explores the important facilitative role that educational developers can play as well as the importance of data to inform such processes. A framework is presented that includes curriculum visioning, curriculum development, and curriculum alignment with course objectives, content, and learning experiences.

In Chapter Three, Dale Roy, Paola Borin, and Erika Kustra present an overview of the literature on organizational change in higher education, along with a detailed description of the centrally administered Learning Innovation Grants Program, which was designed to motivate and support departmental-level curricular and cultural change. In analyzing the success of this program, the authors identify a number of key features, including the importance of having a long-term vision; using a collaborative or consensus-driven approach; focusing more on process (*how* students learn) than outcomes (*what* you'd like them to learn); using a scholarly, data-driven approach; exposing the outcomes to external review; and ensuring adequate support, such as having an embedded consultant.

Chapter Four, by Art Hill, is the first of several chapters that focus on curriculum development processes initiated by faculty. This chapter describes a curriculum development process in a food science department accredited by the Institute of Food Technology. It emphasizes the importance of treating curriculum development as an ongoing process of continuous improvement, as opposed to a one-time event. It also provides an overview of various approaches to curriculum assessment. Perhaps the chapter's most significant contribution is its use of the "learning fractal" as a metaphor for understanding the interrelationships among different levels of curriculum development—namely, the program, individual course, learning module, and classroom experience levels. It effectively integrates this perspective with Kolb and Fry's learning circle.

Chapter Five, by Sharon Mayne Devine, Kerry Daly, Donna Lero, and Claire MacMartin, presents the candid experiences and reflections of a new department chair, an associate department chair, and the faculty cochairs of a committee tasked with developing a new major within a historically significant department whose roots go back over one hundred years. The authors identify a number of lessons learned through the application of the organizational and curriculum change literature to their own experience. These lessons include the importance of cultivating a climate for change; recognizing and managing competing faculty interests; articulating a longer-term vision within which the change will occur; identifying and mobilizing faculty leaders and empowering action; articulating timelines with achievable goals; and recognizing success, consolidating gains, and maintaining momentum.

Chapter Six, by Donna Palmateer Pennee, provides a critical analysis of the challenges faced by the chair of a curriculum committee charged with assessing and developing the core of an interdisciplinary arts and science program. Contributing to these challenges was the program's lack of departmental or college affiliation and the fact that no full-time faculty were assigned to teach in it. The author proposes that a formalized approach to curriculum assessment, along with substantial student involvement, can help make the implicit explicit and, in so doing, illuminate and help to resolve infrastructural, cultural, and systemic issues that can compromise the quality of the development and delivery of curricula.

Chapter Seven, by Pierre Zundell and Thomas Mengel, presents an in-depth examination of a curriculum evolution process used to guide the development of a novel faculty college and one of its most innovative and successful programs—an award-winning Bachelor of Philosophy degree in interdisciplinary leadership studies—with a focus on collaborative, problem-based, experiential, reflective, and active learning. Lessons learned included the need for explicit learning outcomes (both conceptual and operational) reinforced by appropriate organizational values and beliefs, the inclusion of both top-down and bottom-up processes; multiple levels of assessment involving all stakeholders; evidence-based practice (the SoTL); and effective human resource management processes for selecting, engaging, and rewarding faculty.

Chapter Eight, by Frederick Evers and Janet Wolstenholme, similarly presents curriculum development as a process for creating an innovative new educational institution, but in this case it is a joint venture between a university and a college that seeks to fully meet the requirements of both institutions in four years, by integrating theory and practice at the program and course levels. The authors describe the steps taken to identify a comprehensive set of learning objectives, organized as knowledge, skills, and values, to help guide the curriculum development and implementation of six new programs. Examples of innovative learning activities are provided that illustrate the integration of theory and practice. Challenges encountered are briefly discussed, including those associated with navigating curricular reform through the course approval processes of two separate institutions.

Chapter Nine, by Harry Hubball, Neil Gold, Joy Mighty, and Judy Britnell, describes the development and implementation of provincially based degree-level expectations, along with a comprehensive, stage-specific framework—composed of awareness, initiation, mobilization, action, and practice—in support of both externally and internally generated curriculum reform. Lessons learned include the following: effective curriculum development takes a considerable amount of time and resources; the commitment and empowerment of the learning community and key leaders are essential; and educational contexts are inherently complex. These issues, along with well-entrenched barriers to change, such as the attitudes of faculty who are required to reexamine their own courses, can present considerable implementation challenges.

Chapter Ten, by Julia Christensen Hughes, concludes the volume. It suggests that interest in curriculum assessment and development is likely

NEW DIRECTIONS FOR TEACHING AND LEARNING • DOI: 10.1002/tl

to continue to grow and synthesizes the advice for such processes provided in the preceding nine chapters. It also seeks to identify the implications of these recommendations and suggests that the most profound of these are associated with changes to the faculty role. For example, the recommendations have implications for faculty skills and knowledge, development activities, and selection and reward processes. They also suggest that faculty should fully embrace the concept of being a scholar. Finally, there are implications for faculty approaches to course development and delivery. Some may feel that concepts such as academic freedom may be threatened. It is vital to ensure that this freedom is retained.

Julia Christensen Hughes
Peter Wolf
Editors

JULIA CHRISTENSEN HUGHES, PhD, is chair of the Department of Business at the University of Guelph, in Ontario, former director of Teaching Support Services, and past president of the Society for Teaching and Learning in Higher Education (STLHE).

PETER WOLF, MAdEd, is associate director (acting) and manager of Instruction Development of Teaching Support Services at the University of Guelph, in Ontario. He is also on the board of directors of the Institute for the Advancement of Teaching in Higher Education (IATHE).

NEW DIRECTIONS FOR TEACHING AND LEARNING • DOI: 10.1002/tl

1

Scholarly approaches to curriculum practice are critical to the success of undergraduate program reform.

The Scholarship of Curriculum Practice and Undergraduate Program Reform: Integrating Theory into Practice

Harry Hubball, Neil Gold

In a global higher education context of increasing competition for student recruitment, interinstitutional student mobility, credit transfer flexibility, and quality assurance policies, learning outcomes have become part of recent international trends in institutional, curricula, and pedagogical reforms, with profound effects on all aspects of curriculum development, implementation, and evaluation. Forty-five countries in the European Higher Education Union, for example, have recently signed the Bologna Agreement, whose accompanying quality assurance framework in part requires clearly defined program-level learning outcomes in approximately four thousand European institutions by the year 2010 (Australian Government, Department of Education, Science and Training, 2006; Bergen Communiqué, 2005).

Expectations of explicit learning outcomes and assessment policies in undergraduate curricula are also integral criteria established by the Council of Regional Accrediting Commissions (CRAC) in the United States for all seven agencies responsible for state universities and colleges. For example, successful accreditation of U.S. colleges or universities requires them to demonstrate that education is best experienced within a community of learning where competent professionals are actively and cooperatively

NEW DIRECTIONS FOR TEACHING AND LEARNING, no. 112, Winter 2007 © Wiley Periodicals, Inc.
Published online in Wiley InterScience (www.interscience.wiley.com) • DOI: 10.1002/tl.293

involved with creating, providing, and improving the instructional program; learning is dynamic and interactive, regardless of the setting in which it occurs; instructional programs leading to degrees having integrity are organized around substantive and coherent curricula that define expected learning outcomes; institutions accept the obligation to address student needs related to, and to provide the resources necessary for, their academic success; institutions are responsible for the education provided in their name; institutions undertake the assessment and improvement of their quality, giving particular emphasis to student learning; and institutions voluntarily subject themselves to peer review (Eaton, 2007; CRAC, 2003).

Similarly the National Protocols, authorized by the Australian government, are a key element of the national quality assurance framework for Australian higher education. Essentially this framework regulates all higher education institutions (including thirty-eight public funded universities) and their courses to ensure the broad implementation of nationally agreed-upon objectives for Australian higher education (Ministerial Council on Education, Employment Training and Youth Affairs, 2006). In conjunction with the National Protocols, the Learning and Teaching Performance Funding serves to reward Australian higher education institutions that best demonstrate excellence in learning and teaching. This critical funding framework assesses institutions using explicit performance indicators (including learning-centered teaching practices and program-level learning outcomes such as students' demonstration of teamwork skills, problem solving, analytical skills, written communications, and self-directed learning skills) and, on this basis, awards substantial funding using a complex allocation formula (Australian Government Press, 2003; Australian Government, Department of Education, Science and Training, 2006).

Over the last five to ten years in particular, research universities in Canada have afforded special attention to the quality of undergraduate education and the demonstrable attributes of its graduates. More recently at the provincial level in Canada, guidelines have been established for degree-level expectations in Ontario's twenty publicly assisted universities (OCAV Report, 2005). Ontario's degree-level expectations originate from a Minister's Post-secondary Review Report of Higher Education, which recommended that every university in Ontario should implement the National Survey for Student Engagement (NSSE) in 2006–07 (Rae, 2005). The NSSE has been administered in over one thousand universities and colleges in North America and focuses on students' responses to approximately ninety questions pertaining to five broad areas of student engagement: level of academic challenge, active and collaborative learning, student-faculty interactions, enriching educational experiences, and supportive campus environment. The NSSE is widely recognized as providing reliable and valid indicators about the quality of undergraduate degree programs and lasting academic outcomes (National Survey of Student Engagement, 2007). However, despite this recent activity with degree-level expectations, learning outcomes are not a new concept in higher education and are an integral part of diverse as well as contemporary notions of learning-centered undergraduate curricula (Bresciani, 2006; Daniel, 1993; Green, 1999; Mok, 1999).

Situating the Complexities of Undergraduate Curricula

First it is useful to provide an operational definition of learning-centered curriculum in higher education. We refer to curriculum as a coherent program of study (such as a four-year B.Sc.) that is responsive to the needs and circumstances of the pedagogical context and is carefully designed to develop students' knowledge, abilities, and skills through multiple integrated and progressively challenging course learning experiences.

Undergraduate curricula are thus complex and multifaceted processes shaped by many factors (social, political, economic, organizational, cultural, and individual); occur at various stages of development and perhaps reform; and involve people at several institutional levels in the teaching and learning context (administrators, curriculum development committee members and support team, instructors, and students) (Green and Kreuter, 1999; Wiles and Bondi, 2002). Program-level learning outcomes are a central component of learning-centered curricula. Learning outcomes can occur at many different levels (such as professional accreditation, quality assessment reviews, institutional planning, program development, individual course design), in the form of both top-down and bottom-up processing, each of which (and in various combinations) can have significant implications for implementation practices. Figure 1.1 illustrates the complex interconnections of learning outcome contexts.

Figure 1.1. Interconnected Model of Learning Outcomes in Various Undergraduate Program Contexts

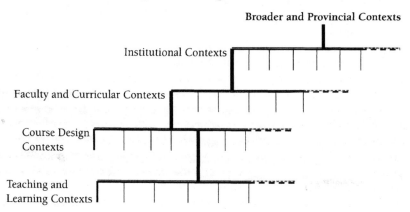

Given this complexity and the many consequential complications, the localized development and declaration of program-level learning outcomes, as well as the careful integration and alignment of these outcomes within the curriculum, can be a major undertaking for most institutions and academic units. Developing, implementing, and evaluating learning-centered curricula are iterative processes that cannot be treated as discrete entities but rather must be carefully integrated. As a result it is imprudent for each entity to be considered the responsibility of completely different people (Diamond, 1998; Ewell, 1997; Fullan, 2001; Hubball and Burt, forthcoming; Ottoson and Green, 1987; Green and Kreuter, 1999; Murphy, 1997).

Traditional approaches to undergraduate programming in higher education, however, are often characterized by well-intentioned, select committees making ad hoc decisions about adding, modifying, or "tinkering" with individual course offerings. Such approaches pay little attention to integration and the scholarship of curriculum practice (SoCP), and they fail to address learning styles and the desirability of devising strategically placed and diverse learning experiences within the curriculum—such as prior learning assessment (PLA), capstone projects, field-based learning, interdisciplinarity, interprofessionalism, internationalization, and the use of learning technologies, simulation, and role playing. These approaches typically rely on students' efforts to make sense of the whole (if at all) from a broad set of often fragmented and unconnected individual course learning experiences. When attention has been afforded to learning outcomes in these contexts, the assessment procedures for measuring students' learning are often narrow, rigid, or at surface level—using, for example, simplistic right-or-wrong quiz questions or isolated behavioral checklists. So even where applied, learning outcomes have had a somewhat checkered past with very mixed reviews and levels of success or satisfaction in higher education (Baron, 1996; Ganderton, 1996; Gibbs, Dunbar-Goddet, Law, and Rust, 2006; Jansen and Christie, 1999).

Learning-Centered Approaches to Undergraduate Curricula: Integrating Theory into Practice

Learning-centered reforms in undergraduate programming are part of a larger process of institutional, curricula, and pedagogical reform in higher education (Barr and Tag, 1995; Hubball and Burt, 2004; Kupperschmidt and Burns, 1997; Parekh, 2007; Schneider and Schoenberg, 1999). The learning-centered curriculum has its pedagogical roots in constructivism and context-based learning theories and places emphasis on learning communities, curriculum cohesion and integration, diverse pedagogies, clearly defined learning outcomes, and the scholarship of curriculum practice (Barab and Duffy, 2000; Ewell, 1997; Gold, 1997; Hansman, 2001; Lave and Wenger, 1991; Wenger, 1998). The underlying assumptions about learning-centered curricula are that representative students, faculty, and stakeholders in the broader context are active participants in the curricular reform process; that academic units are at different stages of curricular reform and will implement reform of curricula in diverse ways; that learning-centered curricula focus on contextually bound learning outcomes and integration of diverse pedagogies; and that learning outcomes focus on higher-order and integrated abilities about what students are expected to know and be able to do (demonstrating, for instance, critical thinking, responsible use of ethical principles, effective research, communication and problem-solving skills) in the context of a field of study, and are designed to be assessable, transferable, and relevant to students' lives as workers and citizens in a diverse world (Baird, 1996; Bresciani, 2006; Clanchy and Ballard, 1995; Cox and Richlin, 2004; Erickson, 2002; Hubball and Poole, 2004; Hubball and Burt, 2004; Kanpol, 1995).

In pragmatic ways, contemporary approaches to learning outcomes inform students about what they can expect to achieve from a program of study so they can organize their time and efforts, prepare for assessment, and see the links between and among segments of a curriculum, thus enhancing transferability of learnings. These approaches communicate curriculum and program goals in a meaningful way to a broader community, help determine the extent to which learning has been accomplished, and guide faculty and administrators (within resource constraints) in part to determine program(s) of study, course objectives, appropriate learning experiences, assessment, and program evaluation strategies (Nichols, 2002). It is important to emphasize that in order to meet the diverse needs and circumstances of undergraduate program contexts, no single implementation strategy or "cookbook" approach to curriculum development will suit all academic settings. Developing, implementing, and evaluating learning-centered curricula is thus a scholarly process. An institutional commitment to research, therefore, will likely improve the quality of undergraduate education and can dovetail with the scholarship of curriculum practice (SoCP).

The Scholarship of Curriculum Practice

Interestingly, while the scholarship of teaching and learning (SoTL) movement and literature have gained considerable recognition and momentum in recent years, much less attention has been afforded to the scholarship of curriculum practice (SoCP). At the very heart of SoCP is an approach to higher education programming that integrates curriculum and pedagogical research in the disciplinary context of a field of study. We introduce SoCP as a new and important concept to the field that contributes to an emerging scholarship on learning-centered undergraduate program reform. When we draw parallels with the SoTL literature, we must make an important distinction between scholarly approaches to curriculum practice and SoCP, although both provide tremendous impetus for the improvement of learning-centered curricula.

NEW DIRECTIONS FOR TEACHING AND LEARNING • DOI: 10.1002/tl

Scholarly approaches to curriculum practice can engage all faculty in reflecting on and initiating positive changes to course design and curriculum practices. Essentially scholarly approaches to curriculum practice are key for understanding student learning; for developing flexible, responsive, cohesive and integrated curricula; and for assessing whether and how curriculum learning experiences are effective at specific stages and in specific circumstances. Action research methodology is central to scholarly approaches to curriculum practice. Action research internalizes theory and practice through a systematic and cyclical process of inquiry that involves hypothesis testing, planning, observing, analysis, and action (Mills, 2000; Peterat and Smith, 2001; Sander and Halas, 2003). Essentially action research invites faculty and curriculum leaders to consider which research questions concerning program development, implementation, and evaluation are important; what data to gather; when and how to collect and analyze these data; how to initiate positive changes to practice; how to engage curriculum stakeholders in the process; and, finally, how this research might be of interest to the broader scholarly community. Data collection strategies from the research may be quantitative, qualitative, or both. Qualitative sources (such as Internet or documentation searches, course syllabi reviews, open-ended feedback forms and interviews, interpretation of teaching performances and learning experiences from video footage, students' assignments, workbook journals, and curriculum meeting notes) can be analyzed by categorizing data according to established criteria, major themes, and common or isolated experiences (Altrichter, Psch, and Somekh, 1993; Lincoln and Guba, 1985; Strauss and Corbin, 1998). Quantitative data sources (such as numeric performance and graduation records, number of learning outcomes and assessment methods, and rating and rank-order preference scales) lend themselves to categorization by descriptive statistics to determine frequency counts, means, and standard deviations or, if appropriate, by using more complex forms of analytical statistics. Appropriate combinations of qualitative and quantitative data can yield critical information to enhance program development, implementation, and evaluation (Bullough and Pinnegar, 2001; Wolf, Hill, and Evers, 2006). Action research, therefore, provides authentic data for use in evaluating the effectiveness of program processes and outcomes (by examining, for example, input from faculty members, practitioners, students, students' work, and course instructors' experiences). It can also engage key stakeholders in the process of further improving the program (Gold, 1997; Thompson, 1996).

The SoCP takes scholarly approaches to curriculum practice to another level of rigor and engagement by disseminating curriculum research in peer review contexts. Thus an operational definition of the SoCP is the ongoing learning and dissemination of practice-driven curricula research in peer review contexts. Three key themes are embedded in this definition: ongoing learning (through reflection, workshops, collaborative and self-directed projects, and literature reviews, for example), practice-driven curricula (focusing on contextually bound issues of programming, courses, classroom experiences, and student learning), and peer review (dissemination of research through curriculum leadership, journal publications, grant writing, and conference presentations, for example). In addition to scholarly approaches to curriculum practice, SoCP has enormous potential for improving student learning because it critically impacts the quality of programming, course structures, and pedagogical experiences in which students learn. Furthermore, SoCP makes a broader scholarly contribution to undergraduate program reform and the enhancement of curriculum practices by raising critical questions for investigation such as these:

What is the purpose of a university, and how do undergraduate curricula serve this purpose?

What theoretical frameworks can inform curriculum practices?

How do perspectives of learning shape curriculum practices?

Who is responsible for undergraduate curricula?

How do programs reconcile quality and quantity of program-level learning outcomes?

How do we actually know that students are able to demonstrate these outcomes on completion of our degree program?

What relationships exist among program development, implementation, and evaluation?

By which means will we judge the quality or effectiveness of undergraduate programs? By learning context, process, impact, long-term follow-up evaluations, or some combination of these?

SoCP is not, however, a panacea for quality undergraduate programming, because of the considerable learning context challenges academic units typically face in developing, implementing, and evaluating learning-centered curricula—challenges such as existing academic workload stress, traditionally low priority for curriculum leadership, curriculum fatigue, or lack of local expertise in SoCP. Thus, when SoCP is combined and integrated with SoTL and the scholarship of educational leadership (SoEL), institutions and academic units are well equipped to engage in learning-centered undergraduate program reform. Consequently, if SoCP is not adequately supported, critical curriculum questions can present significant challenges for many faculty members and administrators. The magnitude of these challenges may become an outright deterrent for some academic units undertaking curriculum change (Drummond, Nixon, and Wiltshire, 1998; Kemp and Seagraves, 1995; Green, 1999; Schneider and Shoenberg, 1999; Shavelson and Huang, 2003). Critical examinations of an undergraduate curriculum should not be relegated to five-year summative data-gathering frenzies for institutional or accreditation reviews. Rather, undergraduate curricula should be considered scholarly, formative, and developmental review processes for all stakeholders in the program learning community. Thus responsibility for SoCP is shared at the institutional, faculty, and student levels. At the institutional level there should be adequate incentives, rewards, and support structures for SoCP. At the faculty level there must be adequate attention to SoCP in the tenure and promotion process, curriculum leadership awards, curriculum excellence awards, curriculum innovation awards, institutional programs that focus on the SoCP, and curriculum support initiatives. At the student level, commitment to SoCP is evident in professional development and the quality of undergraduate programming.

Summary

Higher education organizations, institutions, and academic units globally are grappling with the challenges of redesigning curricula and developing and adopting institutional, professional, and program-level learning outcomes. Implementing learning-centered curricula, however, cannot be considered simply as a series of unproblematic and discrete steps. This special edition journal contributes to a growing body of literature and emerging discourse on philosophical orientations, theoretical concepts, principles, research, and practice implications of SoCP to enhance student learning in higher education.

References

Altrichter, H., Psch, P., and Somekh, B. *Teachers Investigate Their Work: An Introduction to the Methods of Action Research.* London: Routledge, 1993.

Australian Government Press. *Our Universities: Backing Australia's Future Initiative.* Canberra: Government Publications, 2003.

Australian Government, Department of Education, Science and Training. "The Bologna Process and Australia: Next Steps." *Government Ministers' Report Publications,* Apr. 2006.

Baird, L. L. "Documenting Student Outcomes in Graduate and Professional Programs." In A. E. Bilder and C. F. Conrad (eds.), *Challenges in Assessing Outcomes in Graduate and Professional Education.* New Directions for Institutional Research, no. 92. San Francisco: Jossey-Bass, 1996.

Barab, S. A., and Duffy, T. "From Practice Fields to Communities of Practice." In D. Jonassen and S. M. Land (eds.), *Theoretical Foundations of Learning Environments.* Mahwah, N.J.: Erlbaum Associates, 2000.

Baron, M. A. "Dispelling the Myths Surrounding Outcome-Based Education." *Phi Delta Kappan,* 1996, 77(8), 574–576.

Barr, R. B., and Tag, J. "From Teaching to Learning: A New Paradigm for Undergraduate Education." *Change,* 1995, 27(6), 13–25.

Bergen Communiqué. "The European Higher Education Area: Achieving the Goals." Communique of the Conference of European Ministers Responsible for Higher Education. The Bologna Process, Bergen, May 2005.

Bresciani, M. J. *Outcomes-Based Academic and Co-Curricular Program Review.* Sterling, Va.: Stylus, 2006.

Bullough, R., and Pinnegar, S. "Guidelines for Quality in Autobiographical Forms of Self-Study Research." *Educational Researcher,* 2001, 30(3), 13–21.

Clanchy, J., and Ballard, B. "Generic Skills in the Context of Higher Education." *Higher Education Research and Development,* 1995, 14(2), 155–166.

Council of Regional Accrediting Commissions. *Regional Accreditation and Student Learning: Principles of Good Practice.* Washington, D.C.: CRAC, 2003.

Cox, M., and Richlin, L. (eds.) "Building Faculty Learning Communities." New Directions for Teaching and Learning, no. 97. San Francisco: Jossey-Bass, 2004.

Daniel, J. "The Challenge of Mass Education." *Studies in Higher Education,* 1993, *18*(2), 197–203.

Diamond, R. M. *Developing and Assessing Courses and Curricula.* San Francisco: Jossey-Bass, 1998.

Drummond, I., Nixon, I., and Wiltshire, J. "Personal Transferable Skills in Higher Education: The Problems of Implementing Good Practice." *Quality Assurance in Education,* 1998, *6*(1), 44–58.

Eaton, J. "Accreditation and Recognition in the United States." Council of Higher Education Accreditation. *Presidential Report and Guideline Series,* vol. 5, Apr. 2007.

Erickson, L. *Concept-Based Curriculum and Instruction.* Thousand Oaks, Calif.: Corwin Press, 2002.

Ewell, P. J. "Identifying Indicators of Curricular Quality." In G. J. Gaff, L. J. Ratcliff, and Associates (eds.), *Handbook of the Undergraduate Curriculum: A Comprehensive Guide to Purposes, Structures, Practices, and Change.* San Francisco: Jossey-Bass, 1997.

Fullan, M. G. *The New Meaning of Educational Change.* (3rd ed.). New York: Teachers College, Columbia University, 2001.

Ganderton, P. S. "Concepts of Globalisation and Their Impact upon Curriculum Policy Making: Rhetoric and Reality. A Study of Australasian Reform." *International Journal of Educational Development,* 1996, *16*(4), 393–405.

Gibbs, G., Dunbar-Goddet, H., Law, S., and Rust, C. "Characterising Features of Program-Level Assessment Environments That Support Learning." Paper presented at the International Student Learning Conference, Bath, England, Sept. 2006.

Gold, P. "Faculty Collaboration for a New Curriculum." *Liberal Education,* 1997, *83*(1), 46–49.

Green, A. "Education and Globalisation in Europe and E. Asia: Convergent and Divergent Trends." *Journal of Educational Policy,* 1999, *14*(1), 55–71.

Green, L. W., and Kreuter, M. *Health Promotion Planning: An Educational and Ecological Approach.* Palo Alto, Calif.: Mayfield, 1999.

Hansman, C. A. "Context-Based Adult Learning." In S. B. Merriam (ed.), *The New Update on Adult Learning Theory.* San Francisco: Jossey-Bass, 2001.

Hubball, H. T., and Burt, H. D. "Learning Outcomes and Program-Level Evaluation in a Four-Year Undergraduate Pharmacy Curriculum." *American Journal of Pharmaceutical Education,* forthcoming.

Hubball, H. T., and Burt, H. D. "An Integrated Approach to Developing and Implementing Learning-Centred Curricula." *International Journal for Academic Development,* 2004, *9*(1), 51–65.

Hubball, H. T., and Poole, G. "A Learning-Centred Course on University Teaching." *International Journal for Academic Development,* 2004, *8*(2), 11–24.

Jansen, J., and Christie, P. (eds.). *Changing Curriculum: Studies on Outcomes-Based Education in South Africa.* Cape Town: Juta, 1999.

Kanpol, B. "Outcomes-Based Education and Democratic Commitment Hopes and Possibilities." *Educational Policy,* 1995, *9*(4), 359–374.

Kemp, I. J., and Seagraves, L. "Transferable Skills:—Can Higher Education Deliver?" *Studies in Higher Education,* 1995, *20*(3), 315–328.

Kupperschmidt, B. R., and Burns, P. "Curriculum Revision Isn't Just Change: It's Transition!" *Journal of Professional Nursing,* 1997, *13*(2), 90–98.

Lave, J., and Wenger, E. *Situated Learning: Legitimate Peripheral Participation.* New York: Cambridge University Press, 1991.

Lincoln, Y. S., and Guba, E. G. *Naturalistic Inquiry.* Beverly Hills, Calif.: Sage, 1985.

Mills, G. E. *Action Research: A Guide for the Teacher Researcher.* Upper Saddle River, N.J.: Merrill Prentice Hall, 2000.

Ministerial Council on Education, Employment Training and Youth Affairs. *Revised National Protocols for Higher Education Approval Process.* Brisbane Report, Australian Government Press, July 2006.

Mok, K. H. "Education and the Marketplace in Hong Kong and Mainland China." *Higher Education,* 1999, *37,* 133–158.

Murphy, S. E. "Eight Components of Program Implementation." *Performance Improvement,* 1997, *36*(1), 6–8.

National Survey of Student Engagement. 2007. Retrieved from http://nsse.iub.edu.

Nichols, J. O. *A Practitioner's Handbook for Institutional Effectiveness and Student Outcomes Assessment Implementation.* New York: Agathon Press, 2002.

OCAV Report. "Working Group on University Undergraduate Degree Level Expectations." Ontario Council of Academic Vice-Presidents, Oct. 24, 2005. Retrieved from http://72.14.253.104/search?q=cache:gsQ9IKN9NDMJ:www.uwo.ca/univsec/handbook/general/OCAV_Guidelines_2005.pdf+Ontario+Council+of+Academic+Vice-Presidents&hl=en&gl=ca&ct=clnk&cd=3.

Ottoson, J. M., and Green, L. W. "Reconciling Concept and Context: Theory of Implementation." *Advances in Health Education and Promotion,* 1987, *2,* 353–382.

Parekh, B. "Fighting the War on Dogma." *Canadian Association of University Teachers Bulletin,* Jan. 2007, *54,* 1.

Peterat, L., and Smith, M. G. "In-forming Practice Through Classroom Inquiry." In L. Peterat and M. G. Smith (eds.), *In-forming Practice Through Action Research: Yearbook 21.* Peoria, Ill.: American Association for Family and Consumer Sciences and Glencoe/McGraw-Hill, 2001.

Rae, R. *The Ontario Post-secondary Review.* 2005. http://www.gov.on.ca.

Sander, N., and Halas, J. "Action Research as Responsible Practice: Parental Responses to Assessment, Evaluation, and Reporting Practices in Physical Education." *Physical and Health Education Journal,* Summer 2003, pp. 12–17.

Schneider, C. G., and Shoenberg, R. "Habits Hard to Break: How Persistent Features of Campus Life Frustrate Curricular Reform." *Change,* Mar.–Apr. 1999, pp. 30–35.

Shavelson, R., and Huang, L. "Responding Responsibly to the Frenzy to Assess Learning in Higher Education." *Change,* Jan.–Feb. 2003, pp. 11–18.

Strauss, A., and Corbin, J. *Basics of Qualitative Research: Techniques and Procedures for Developing Grounded Theory.* (2nd ed.). Thousand Oaks, Calif.: Sage, 1998.

Thompson, S. "How Action Research Can Put Teachers and Parents on the Same Team." *Educational Horizons,* 1996, *74*(2), 70–76.

Wenger, E. *Communities of Practice.* Cambridge, U.K.: Cambridge University Press, 1998.

Wiles, J., and Bondi, J. *Curriculum Development: A Guide to Practice.* (6th ed.) Upper Saddle River, N.J.: Merrill Prentice Hall, 2002.

Wolf, P., Hill, A., and Evers, F. *A Handbook for Curriculum Assessment.* Guelph, Ont.: University of Guelph Publications, 2006.

HARRY HUBBALL *is associate professor in the Department of Curriculum Studies at the University of British Columbia. His research interests focus on the scholarship of curriculum and pedagogical practice in university contexts.*

NEIL GOLD *is vice president academic and provost at the University of Windsor, Canada. He is a member of the Ontario Council of Academic Vice-Presidents.*

NEW DIRECTIONS FOR TEACHING AND LEARNING • DOI: 10.1002/tl

2

This chapter explores the processes that have been developed and refined by educational developers in Teaching Support Services at the University of Guelph to support faculty-driven curriculum assessment and development initiatives.

A Model for Facilitating Curriculum Development in Higher Education: A Faculty-Driven, Data-Informed, and Educational Developer–Supported Approach

Peter Wolf

In the fall of 2003, Teaching Support Services (TSS), a department at the University of Guelph, was approached by a faculty member in the department of food sciences. Professor Art Hill was interested in seeking support in systematically assessing the department's undergraduate curriculum and using that assessment to trigger further improvement of the program curriculum. This was one of the first times that TSS was included in a program-level teaching and learning initiative at the University of Guelph. Previously most of the work of the center involved supporting individual educators in improving their often isolated courses through, for example, access to higher education literature, informed pedagogical practices, and course design processes.

The success of this first project has led to many others. Over the past few years, TSS has supported many programs, departments, colleges, faculties, and the university as a whole by developing a flexible, data-driven

The author would like to recognize Trevor Holmes for his support in the development of the curriculum evolution processes and in the preparation of this article. His thanks also go to Louise McIntyre for her administrative support.

approach to fostering a continuous improvement process in curriculum development. Since this time, the center has reoriented its educational development capacity to make room for the growing demand for support in the assessment and development of curricula.

The support offered has broadened from helping Professor Hill develop systematic and comprehensive curriculum assessment processes to include curriculum visioning, mapping, and a variety of activities that foster the engagement of faculty in scholarly and comprehensive efforts to evolve curriculum in meaningful ways.

Our curriculum development approach can best be described as faculty-driven, data-informed, and educational development–supported. Aware of prior practical and theoretical work on curriculum development, alignment, and assessment—in particular Diamond (1998), Gaff and Ratcliff (1996), and Biggs (1999)—we wanted to build on a culture that relies on expert disciplinary knowledge and data to make decisions to engage faculty members in a reflective process that they use to foster continuous improvement in curriculum. We also wanted to make explicit the links between student perceptions, student learning and assessment approaches, faculty goals for students and for their program, alumni success, and employer and society needs.

The Curriculum Development Model

Figure 2.1 depicts the processes used by faculty in efforts to systematize the curriculum development. The term *curriculum development* implies that curricula develop by a continuous process. This is in opposition to the commonly used *curriculum renewal,* which seems to imply episodic attempts to develop curriculum.

Curriculum Visioning. A common impetus or catalyst for many curriculum development initiatives comes from the faculty who are interested in improving their curriculum so as to benefit student learning. Often this notion will start with an assessment of the curriculum. At Guelph, in this phase, an assessment strategy is developed using Kirkpatrick's four levels of evaluation (1998) as a framework for choosing inputs. Data are gathered from relevant stakeholders such as alumni, graduating students, entering students, and employers. Working with the faculty (most often the program committee) that has taken on the responsibility for curriculum development, a strength, weakness, opportunities, and threats (SWOT) summary chart is developed. At a program retreat that usually includes faculty, administration, and graduate students, a separate SWOT is developed. This SWOT—in combination with other data like previous reviews, existing program objectives, and information from other similar programs—is then collectively interpreted. From this retreat comes a series of recommended actions, which often include a variety of issues—from logistical issues (such as insufficient courses in *x* year), to marketing issues (such as increasing enrollment through better promotion), to teaching development issues (such as teach-

NEW DIRECTIONS FOR TEACHING AND LEARNING • DOI: 10.1002/tl

Figure 2.1. Curriculum Development: Process Overview

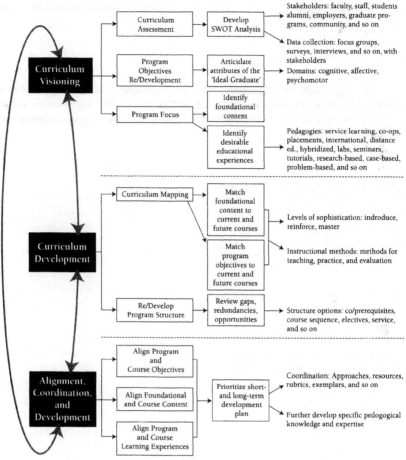

Copyright © Peter Wolf, University of Guelph, 2007.

ing assistant training). The data have almost always shown that on balance the program has considerable strengths, and this evidence reassures departments that much of what they do is recognized by stakeholders as effective and worthwhile.

The main focus of the retreat, often facilitated by the educational developer, is to examine or to reexamine program objectives developed in the language of the attributes of the ideal graduate. To support this effort, the educational developers at TSS have a variety of models on hand to help inform the discussions, and these have been adapted to reflect discipline-based goals in program-based contexts (Evers, Rush, and Berdrow, 1998;

University of Guelph Learning Objectives, 1987; Ontario Council of Academic Vice Presidents, 2005). Also articulated (or rearticulated) is the key content—the "walk-around" knowledge that is considered foundational to the discipline. Most often participants coming away from this retreat find a shared commitment to connecting courses with the program objectives in an increasingly intentional and systematic way, with increasing levels of complexity as students move through the program.

Curriculum Development. In this phase, the focus is on collecting data from the course instructors on how they are choosing (or not choosing) to foster student development in identified program objectives and foundational content. Using commercial customized software, instructors volunteer information on each identified program objective separately (including those based on key content areas), identifying the percentage of effort that is spent on developing each, the level of sophistication sought, and the methods for teaching, learning, and assessment used. Once gathered, the data can be fully analyzed with the spreadsheet software. The data are interpreted by the program committee, often with an educational developer sitting as an ad hoc committee member.

The summary generally identifies the major approaches to teaching and assessing the major content and skills development areas and typically identifies which program objectives are currently being fostered effectively and which are not. It takes into account the curriculum assessment, if one was conducted.

The summary is then presented at a second faculty retreat. Here the faculty discuss the results, establish priorities, and determine courses of action.

Alignment, Coordination, and Development. This retreat leads into Phase 3—Alignment, Coordination and Development—where many actions can take place based on the priorities set. Follow-up activities have included volunteer groups of faculty working together with the educational developer, reviewing the literature and research on one or more program objectives, developing relevant rubrics and exemplars of differing levels of skill development, and developing suggested teaching approaches to foster skill development. These are then presented to the department where faculty volunteer their courses to be integrated with other courses in the development of the objective. Other courses can formally or informally adopt the rubric, exemplars, and teaching approaches to further support student development.

Other follow-up activities have included the development and delivery of customized workshops (such as fostering student information literacy across the program) or encouraging attendance at relevant TSS or external workshops, institutes, and conferences.

The set of actions chosen will set the curriculum development agenda for the subsequent two to three years, with regular reports back to the faculty on developments, challenges, and successes. After the initiatives have been implemented, a follow-up meeting is held to discuss assessing the

NEW DIRECTIONS FOR TEACHING AND LEARNING • DOI: 10.1002/tl

effectiveness, efficiency, adequacy, and appropriateness of the efforts made and the actual outcomes.

Attributes of the Curriculum Development Model. The faculty-driven, data-informed educational development supported process described here fosters a culture in which faculty explore program objectives and their outcomes regularly. The attributes key to its impact are described below.

Start with at least one faculty "champion." The key to engaging curriculum evolution processes is at least one program faculty member who is willing to drive the process; to work within the program to engage faculty; to help design, collect, and interpret data; and often facilitate the retreats. Quite often this person is the chair of the program curriculum committee, and it is through this person that the committee often begins actively championing curriculum evolution processes.

Engage a curriculum facilitator or educational developer. Accessing an educational developer to support faculty-driven curriculum evolution processes can be extremely beneficial. Some of the key benefits to naming an outside educational developer as facilitator include added expertise in course design, awareness of the curriculum practices in diverse disciplines and contexts, familiarity with higher education–related teaching and learning theories and practices, and an ability to act as facilitator, change agent, and coach.

Educational developers skilled at supporting faculty-driven, data-driven curriculum development processes are careful not to walk into departments armed with experts' books or worksheets. Rather, attending to Bath, Smith, Stein, and Swann (2004) on the "validated and living curriculum" as well as Knight (2001) on complexity and process, educational developers work to help make explicit outcomes over which all constituencies can claim ownership, rather than forcing a systematized outcome-based approach. As Knight (2001) puts it, we aim "to provide ingredients from which a meal can be created, rather than to insist on cooking to a recipe" (p. 375).

Ensure that the process stays on track and moves forward. The primary tasks for the educational developer are to encourage respectful consideration of diverse perspectives, bring an awareness of local and broader cultural issues or opportunities, offer expertise in a broad range of curriculum and education-related approaches, and provide access to the research literature. Striking the balance between staying neutral in process facilitation while promoting scholarly approaches to teaching and learning in higher education is a formidable challenge.

Use data as a foundation for development. The data coming from both the curriculum assessment and from the mapping processes engage faculty in meaningful ways, even if the quantitative data is sometimes critiqued as statistically invalid due to, for example, too small a sample size. The value of data in providing a snapshot prompts scholarly discussions that can then prompt investigation into scholarly literature, attendance at conference presentations, and discussions with colleagues outside the program. These activities can then lead to contextually innovative and well-grounded curriculum choices.

Engage curriculum development as a continuous improvement process. It has taken programs up to one year to complete all of the phases of this model, often in stops and starts as the routines of the academic year dictate. Once ideas are implemented, assessing and adapting the implementation begin, followed some time afterwards by the next full-scale curriculum assessment.

Certainly most of the programs that have engaged in the processes described here have not worked through all the phases. Some have sought support with just one phase considered in isolation. Engaging in any of the curriculum evolution phases often sets the stage for the next phase.

Engaging in curriculum development processes helps to foster a program culture that regularly and rigorously examines its curriculum. We think our approach works because it provides enough instructional design expertise on a just-in-time basis for faculty to develop their own capacity to move to their own next level of curriculum and course alignment in a context of complexity.

References

Bath, D., Smith, C., Stein, S. and Swann, R. "Beyond Mapping and Embedding Graduate Attributes: Bringing Together Quality Assurance and Action Learning to Create a Validated and Living Curriculum." *Higher Education Research and Development,* 2004, 23(3), 313–328.

Biggs, J. *Teaching for Quality Learning at University.* Buckingham, U.K.: SRHE and Open University Press, 1999.

Diamond, R. M. *Designing Courses and Curricula.* San Francisco: Jossey-Bass, 1998.

Evers, F., Rush, J., and Berdrow, I. *The Bases of Competence: Skills for Lifelong Learning and Employability.* San Francisco: Jossey-Bass, 1998.

Gaff, J. G., and Ratcliff, J. L. (eds.) *Handbook of the Undergraduate Curriculum.* San Francisco: Jossey-Bass, 1996.

Kirkpatrick, D. *Evaluating Training Programs: The Four Levels.* San Francisco: Berrett-Koehler, 1998.

Knight, P. T. "Complexity and Curriculum: A Process Approach to Curriculum-Making." *Teaching in Higher Education,* 2001, 6(3), 369–381.

Ontario Council of Academic Vice Presidents. "Guidelines for University Undergraduate Degree Level Expectations." 2005. Retrieved May 20, 2007, from www.tss.uoguelph.ca/id/Degreelevelexp.pdf.

University of Guelph Learning Objectives. 1987. Retrieved May 20, 2007, from www.uoguelph.ca/registrar/calendars/undergraduate/current/c02/c02learningobjectives.shtml.

PETER WOLF, MAdEd, is associate director (acting) and manager of Instruction Development of Teaching Support Services at the University of Guelph, in Ontario. He is also on the board of directors of the Institute for the Advancement of Teaching in Higher Education (IATHE).

3

This chapter describes the assumptions and principles for good practice based on case studies at a research-intensive university in which several departments introduced curriculum change through a novel departmental grants program.

Assisting Curriculum Change Through Departmental Initiatives

Dale Roy, Paola Borin, Erika Kustra

What factors encourage and sustain enduring curriculum change at a typical North American university? Like many faculty members and groups working in teaching and learning centers, we have been concerned with understanding how curriculum change takes place in a university. Our group, the Centre for Leadership in Learning at McMaster University, has been involved in many initiatives intended to bring about change in individual courses, and several attempts to improve undergraduate education at an institutional level. In this chapter we share what we have learned about influencing departmental thinking around sustainable curriculum change and teaching, including a series of insights that may be useful to others treading a similar path.

Before turning to curriculum change through departmental initiatives, it might be useful to look at two other levels at which curriculum change takes place.

Curriculum changes at the course level. Many teaching and learning centers offer assistance to individual faculty members who want to make changes at the course level. However, when a course is assigned to a new instructor, the new instructor's ideas inspire a new version of the course. This approach to curriculum change is less likely to foster incremental improvement. Grants awarded to individual instructors offer tremendous support for inspired faculty, but are less helpful in building a coherent, sustainable curriculum (Sell and Lounsberry, 1997).

NEW DIRECTIONS FOR TEACHING AND LEARNING, no. 112, Winter 2007 © Wiley Periodicals, Inc.
Published online in Wiley InterScience (www.interscience.wiley.com) • DOI: 10.1002/tl.295

Curriculum changes at the institutional level. Approximately nine years ago we shifted focus from course-level changes (with local effects) to campuswide curriculum initiatives. Our first campuswide initiative was an attempt to weave inquiry into the undergraduate curriculum. This effort was enabled with external funding (a McConnell Family Foundation grant), the support of three deans, the support of an enthusiastic vice president, and the interest of a diverse group of faculty members. We created new first-year courses in three faculties—science, social sciences, and humanities—with each course shaped by the knowledge and expertise of the discipline. At the core, each course aimed to develop the skills of conducting inquiry (Boyer Commission on Educating Undergraduates in the Research University, 1998) using a structure-of-the-disciplines model. This model proposes that the subject matter of a discipline is ever-evolving and that each discipline conducts inquiry in a unique way (Bruner, 1960; Posner, 2004). Each faculty developed and offered its own year one inquiry course. The resulting courses met with considerable success, earning both local and national prizes for curriculum design. It seemed there were processes that could bring about significant and lasting change in how people teach—changes that would turn up in other courses they taught. Though the change was initiated centrally, it was clearly important that the change was guided and championed from within the disciplines—created, owned, and evolved by the disciplines themselves.

Unfortunately work on curriculum at the institutional level creates curriculum that sits outside the normal structures of the university, and so necessary support for the curriculum can sometimes fall through the cracks. For example, department chairs routinely staff departmental offerings, but who staffs a university-wide course? Staffing these courses depended on negotiating sessions with department chairs, most of whom had pressing departmental needs to address. Or again we discovered that these university-wide courses were not subject to the normal student rating process, simply because student ratings were administered by academic departments, and the inquiry courses did not belong to any particular academic department. For these and other reasons (Roy, 2007) we sought to explore the potential of curriculum change through departmental initiatives.

Curriculum changes at the departmental level. We believe curriculum change is more likely to be significant and lasting if it grows out of a departmental consensus. This trend prevails because departments largely own the curriculum and are the seat of many budgetary decisions (Dickeson, 1999). We decided to test this notion by offering curriculum grants to academic departments. We developed a new Departmental Learning Innovation Grants Program, which built on our experience with curriculum change at the institutional level and which encouraged transformation of a department's curriculum.

NEW DIRECTIONS FOR TEACHING AND LEARNING • DOI: 10.1002/tl

In the remaining sections of this chapter, we first summarize some of the literature that is relevant to initiating curriculum change, then we describe the program itself, and finally we list key learnings useful to others working to change curriculum through a departmental initiative.

How Do You Facilitate Change in Higher Education?

Many researchers have examined the entrails of successful and unsuccessful change attempts, poking and prodding in an effort to identify clear and consistent signs to predict what works and what does not. In the end, most strategists fall into some variation of the four categories identified by Jack Lindquist in *Strategies for Change* (1978), an excellent overview for higher education. Lindquist identified a series of strategies likely familiar to those working in universities: rational planning, social interaction, human problem solving, and political approaches to change. As you will see, our own program borrowed from all of these strategies.

Rational planning assumes that a well-developed plan based on evidence and reason will lead to change, though it acknowledges other factors may have influence. Certainly in institutions where research is conducted and evidence emphasized, we would hope for rational planning. However, we know a superbly rational and elegantly reasoned plan will crumple when status and security are threatened, or if the group is not committed.

Social interaction views change as initiated and propagated through social interaction and networks. This perspective draws on research on the diffusion of innovation through groups: innovators, early adopters, early majority, late majority, and laggards (Rogers and Shoemaker, 1971). It underlines the importance of champions, or opinion leaders, in promoting change. In the end, however, change initiatives can still fail as a result of insufficient training, insufficient perceived benefit, or the perception of onerous effort.

The resolution of human problems strategy addresses psychological components by identifying obstacles to change and dealing with resistance. This approach begins with the world of the user. User need is turned into a problem statement, someone from the outside helps to plan and implement the change, and internal knowledge and resources are weighted at least equally with external knowledge and resources. Finally, it suggests that lasting change and the best motivation are brought about when the process is initiated by the user or client group.

The final approach is very familiar in any large organization. When all else fails, the most common approach is the use of political power. This strategy employs authoritative decisions to require compliance.

More recently, John Kotter (1996) identified eight steps to bring about successful change. He suggested a need to first establish a sense of urgency, create a coalition, and develop a clear vision. The next steps are to share the vision, empower people to clear obstacles, and secure short-term wins.

The final steps require consolidating, continuing movement, and anchoring the change.

All of these models reinforced our thinking and helped shape our efforts to promote lasting curriculum development at the department level. When later in this chapter we discuss the factors we think encourage lasting curriculum change, you will see that we have translated some of this research into very specific actions—for example, we translated the rational planning principle into very detailed requirements for planned curriculum change through departmental grants, or we required curriculum change to be based on a departmental consensus, thereby requiring the very social interaction suggested above.

Encouraging Departmental Curriculum Change: A Novel Grant Program

Like many teaching and learning centers, we offer grants to individual faculty members to enhance a single course. Instructors develop well-reasoned designs for individual courses based on good practice, which changes the mind-set of the instructors as they undergo the paradigm shift from teaching to learning (Barr and Tagg, 1995). Through individual course transformation, we see both instructor enthusiasm and student satisfaction increase. However, when the course is assigned to a new instructor, changes are usually lost. Even large program curriculum changes that rely on the enthusiasm of one individual tend to decline or disappear when the key individual leaves.

Consequently, a course-based approach to curriculum change is less likely to foster incremental improvement and leads to a series of courses, each developed anew with every successive instructor (Sell and Lounsberry, 1997). While helpful for individuals, these grants are less helpful in influencing the broader curriculum. Individuals may, and frequently do, claim ownership of courses, but departments own curricula and are the important location for many other decisions (Dickeson, 1999). Significant curriculum change therefore requires departmental consensus.

We therefore designed curriculum innovation grants for academic departments. Each successful Learning Innovation Grant supports a departmental project for a period up to three years, with a total budget of approximately $100,000 (sponsored by the Imperial Oil Charitable Foundation), a sum large enough to attract the attention of many academic departments. The first step in the process invites interested departments to contact us at the Centre for Leadership in Learning, to provide feedback and some assistance in the design of their projects. Applicants are encouraged to follow three guiding principles (Chickering and Gamson, 1987):

1. Collaboration
2. Scholarly approach to teaching
3. Good practice in teaching

NEW DIRECTIONS FOR TEACHING AND LEARNING • DOI: 10.1002/tl

We particularly encourage projects that support the university focus on developing self-directed learning. The second step requests departments to submit a brief application, from five to ten pages long, including a description of the project, a plan for assessment and dissemination, and a budget. In the third step, applications are reviewed externally, by a panel of experienced teachers. The most promising applications are encouraged to pursue their projects by responding to reviewers' questions and comments. Eight departments are now at varying degrees of completion (Roy and Day, 1999b).

Factors Encouraging Departmental Curriculum Change

The following list of guidelines flows from our experience. Sometimes the literature on curriculum change (mentioned earlier in this chapter) offered us a framework for expressing these guidelines, but often insights emerged from reflection on our experience and discussion among the authors. Some of the principles listed below look as if they apply only to a curriculum grants program, but this is misleading. For example, we argue that substantial curriculum change should be externally reviewed. In our case, this occurred when we sent the departmental grant applications out for external review, but in the absence of grants we would still suggest departments send their proposed curriculum changes out for external review. The benefits of external review apply whether or not grants are involved. In other words, we used the grants program to embed our notions of good practice in curriculum change, but we would argue for the same principles even if no grants were involved.

1. Change is enhanced by developing a long-term vision. The long-term vision for the departmental grants program was documented in our center's McMaster Active Learning Project (Roy and Day, 1999a), influenced by educational literature and the specific university mission and culture. Additionally, in the process of applying for a Departmental Innovation Grant, each department is required to develop a long-term vision customized for their own department. Curriculum change takes time to develop and implement. We found that changes set in a context extending beyond one year were more likely to be enduring (Kotter, 1996; Lindquist, 1978).

2. Lasting curriculum change is not the work of an individual. Significant curriculum change requires departmental consensus (Lindquist, 1978). If we accept the importance of a coalition in which people work together as a team toward a united goal (Kotter, 1996), then how can you ensure this form of consensus exists within a department?

Our experience suggests some form of departmental consensus exists when nearly everyone in the department has a current awareness of the proposed new curriculum and its rationale and can state clearly their own specific role in bringing about the change or in sustaining the change. This clarity allows for varying degrees of participation in the project, but does not leave room for anyone to stand completely idle. To introduce communication skills into the curriculum a department may, for example, have two or three instructors who will design and teach a course in this area. But if there is a departmental consensus, all other instructors in the department should be able to say how their particular courses will support this change, such as providing more opportunities for their students to make class presentations.

3. Curriculum change is increased when respected, experienced colleagues play key roles. The strength of the consensus is suggested by the rank and status of those involved in the project (Rogers and Shoemaker, 1971). The current or more recent chair of the department is usually actively involved, supportive, and an early adopter of the change. In the department proposing to develop better communication skills (for example), the chair might be the first to propose an alteration in a course and be an early adopter of the new curriculum.

4. Successful consensus usually has a history. Real consensus takes time to build. What would a history of consensus look like? In successful cases, a variety of members in a department have been thinking and talking about the proposed change for more than a year. They have collected data on their students and on the results of the curriculum in its current form, and these results have been reviewed and critiqued at departmental meetings and retreats. The greater the number of departmental members involved in these historical activities, the more likely a proposed new curriculum will represent a consensus.

The more successful departmental initiatives have included a plan for maintaining consensus throughout the life of the project. In one case, every member of the department was scheduled to play a role in the change. In other cases, the project was made a regular item in all departmental meetings, so updates were frequent and consistent. These regularly scheduled updates no doubt created pressure for continuous progress on the project and provided a forum for sustaining the departmental consensus over the life of the project.

5. Curriculum change is more enduring if it focuses on *how* students learn, rather than *what* they learn. The focus is on changing the process of teaching and learning rather than on changing only the content. We think this principle is powerful because changing specific content is familiar to faculty and does not usually require important changes on the part of the teacher. If we think of teaching as telling, then changing the curriculum content becomes telling a new story. While a change in the story is important, it does not seem to have the same impact as a decision to change how students learn. For example, a department introducing field work as a new central component of their curriculum will experience a more profound change than one deciding to replace one standard specialty course with another.

There may be an important exception to this rule, as several departments did experience lasting change when they introduced skills into their curriculum. It seems that introducing skills was sufficiently removed from the more familiar content changes that it required significant and important changes in instructor behavior. Once skills are a part of the curriculum, a whole new set of questions arises, including questions about assessment and how to provide coached feedback on skills. Skills also affect how students learned in other areas, perhaps moving students and teachers from working with declarative knowledge, where students know about things, to functioning knowledge, where students also know how and when to do things (Biggs, 1999).

6. Change works best when several departments are working simultaneously at different stages. Though individual departments own their curriculum project, they do not need to work in isolation; in fact, it is better when several departments are working on curriculum change. We awarded two or more departmental grants each year and encouraged groups to share information and resources. Occasionally departments shared tools, such as deep and surface-learning inventories, or strategies, such as the use of exit interviews, or ideas for spending money wisely, such as the extensive use of students as summer assistants.

We held public forums where departments with earlier projects shared their thinking and experience with those considering or just starting a departmental project. Sometimes the public discussions resulted in departments putting forward a new project or withdrawing their proposals for revision. Campus awareness developed about the projects underway and their benefits. Those just getting started could look to the others to imagine the next stage of their own project.

One unanticipated benefit of several teams working on curriculum projects was that groups engaged in a subtle form of competition. Early groups mentored later groups and inspired them to develop better plans and to imagine new possibilities (Rogers and Shoemaker, 1971). Each department wanted their project to be a bit better than their neighboring department.

If your own campus does not currently have a pool of projects on which departments can collaborate, individual departments can connect with departments in their discipline at other universities that have just been through important curriculum change. Curriculum change is a path best trod in the company of others. Those farther along can provide inspiration, leadership, and detailed models for others to follow.

7. Curriculum change is more successful when grounded in the scholarship of teaching and learning. We required all proposals to base their work in educational literature and build in methods for evaluating change. This made prima facie sense but it also had a number of side effects. One difficulty in opening up the curriculum to change is that the curriculum discussion very quickly becomes centered on the need for discipline subspecialties. One cannot do undergraduate chemistry without studying organic chemistry or thermodynamics, and so on. Grounding the debates in the scholarship of teaching shifts these debates into a less familiar arena and provides an opportunity for a fresh approach. The new question framing the debate might become: How can we strike the best balance among teaching knowledge, skills, and attitudes in our curriculum? This type of debate leaves all members of the department free to contribute without concern to protect their particular area of disciplinary expertise.

The requirement of a scholarly approach had a second effect; namely, the provision of an opportunity for several faculty members to look systematically at the scholarship of teaching. It became clear to these faculty members that there was a literature in this area and that questions of curriculum efficacy were open to investigation in ways very similar to questions that arise in their discipline. Each discipline was attracted to the tools that were familiar: in the social sciences they were drawn to survey instruments and focus groups, whereas in the sciences they were more likely to be drawn to benchmarks and pre- and post-testing. For these faculty it turned out that some teaching and learning issues were interest worthy and open to serious and systematic inquiry. Once stimulated by interesting questions about teaching and learning, several faculty members continued to use a scholarly approach to address subsequent questions in their own courses.

The final reason for insisting on a scholarly approach has to do with the literature on the diffusion of innovation (Lindquist, 1978; Rogers and Shoemaker, 1971). We wanted successful curriculum change to stimulate others to initiate changes, and we knew that the key actors are those faculty members who are open to change but need to see the evidence of its value. Innovators at the front of the change curve need no inspiration, and the late majority comes largely out of fear of being left behind. The key to the diffusion of an innovation is therefore the early majority (about 35 percent of the population) who will adopt an innovation or change, but will do so only if it is clear that it is beneficial. Curriculum change can only become rooted if the evidence of its efficacy is ready and available when choices need to be made. A scholarly approach to curriculum innovation held the promise of providing that evidence when needed.

8. A history of a scholarly approach to teaching increases the likelihood of success. Some departments seemed more experienced with building curriculum around real information such as student data, course evaluations, and educational literature. As a consequence, these departments were better able to direct their efforts from the start. For example, they knew from a history of employer interviews that students were graduating without certain key skills. Or again, through a careful survey of field placements, they knew the undergraduate field experience was not providing the expected student learning opportunities. The historical data also provided a potential indicator of success, since they were used as a baseline against which the effect of changes in the curriculum were compared.

When departments did not have such a history, we encouraged the use of pilot projects that involved collecting baseline data. The departmental research could involve looking inward (what is currently happening in our program?) or outward (what are some of the interesting curriculum innovations taking place elsewhere?).

9. Plans for curriculum change should be externally reviewed. External review freed us to coach the applicants and meant that the decision process was not subject to local forces. We chose external reviewers who had administrative experience in other universities and national recognition for teaching skill and educational leadership.

There were several additional benefits to the use of external reviewers. They almost always had good suggestions from their own experience, and those suggestions strengthened every project that went forward. They lent credibility to the process and helped convince some departments they were onto something really important—after all, a group of external experts had certified the proposal as grant-worthy. Finally, the external reviewers were one of several vehicles for telling other universities about the curriculum change efforts at McMaster, a first step in the dissemination requirement of the grants.

10. An embedded consultant is needed to assist with the process of curriculum revision. Departments can benefit from someone outside of the department bringing in new ideas and ways of thinking about the curriculum. The human problem-solving strategy (Lindquist, 1978) to change advocates skilled intervention of some kind to address the obstacles to change and to deal with human resistance. Sometimes the consultant brings a process for reflecting on the curriculum (a matrix of skills, content, and course possibilities), and sometimes the consultant needs to provide an opportunity for people to express their enthusiasm for new possibilities. The consultant can coach the process of building a good project in the proposal stage and can help departments build a strong application for funding. This kind of departmental change we are talking about here is not very widespread, and few departments have all the experience they need to bring about the sort of curriculum transformation envisioned. An embedded consultant can offer encouragement, support, and strategies on an ongoing basis, right through to dissemination of the project results.

11. Curriculum change is enhanced when there is stability in the personnel involved in instituting and maintaining the initial changes. Departmental curriculum initiatives stumble for a variety of reasons. A good project design and rational planning are no guarantee of a successful outcome. While a sound project proposal contains a promising blueprint, actual conditions in a department (such as a retirement, an illness, or a maternity leave) can challenge the best of plans. Successful departments assigned a team of two or three to lead the project, so that one could step out without threatening the project as a whole.

12. Disciplinary differences may lead to different needs for support. Some elements of the change process resonate more quickly with some departments. Key elements of this model (consensus-driven, scholarly, change in how students learn) achieved a quick fit in science, but other faculties typically made fewer applications and had less success. It is difficult to determine the source of this uneven appeal. It may be the result of paradigm differences between disciplines. Science commonly uses an experimental paradigm including observation, hypothesis development, intervention, and the measurement of change, all of which transfer more easily to the curriculum change model required in our application process.

Departments need different kinds of support getting into the literature, designing their projects, or writing a grant application that will receive a favorable review. Several early applications did not understand the emphasis on changes in *how* students learn and so built complex plans for changing *what* they learned. Writing a grant application takes skill, particularly if you are writing in an unfamiliar area, for review by an unfamiliar panel. Using an external review process allowed us to coach the application process and to help candidates with curriculum development.

We learned that you cannot assume uniformity across campus in these areas:

- Departmental knowledge and skill in writing proposals
- Departmental resources in terms of time, personnel, educational interest, educational expertise, and teaching enthusiasm
- Department familiarity with the scholarship of teaching and learning

Consequently those departments most in need of curriculum revision or financial support for curricular revision may not submit proposals. We sought to address the balance by visiting chairs of departments to explain the criteria of the grants program. All were aware of the program, but the visits helped to illustrate the variety of possible curriculum changes and built enthusiasm. The visits resulted in a few pilot projects, a stream of proposals from departments new to the process, and a successful project application. It is clear that this individualized support for departments is important.

The Role of Individual Faculty Members

We have argued that lasting curriculum change is more likely to occur when it is departmentally based and flows from a departmental consensus. If this is so, what can an individual faculty member contribute?

An individual faculty member can choose to play the role of *initiator.* In this role, the instructor begins discussions, invites others to join, suggests ideas, introduces new resources, or invites external speakers from other departments engaged in interesting curriculum practices. Initiators can act as champions for change themselves or find people in positions of power who are able to act as champions. These activities aim to initiate and then sustain interest. For example, in one department a faculty member made curriculum development item of discussion for each departmental meeting. In this way, she invited the entire department to engage in the discussions over an extended period of time and was surprised at many of the unexpected responses of support.

An alternative to the role of initiator is that of *implementer.* In this role, the faculty member chooses to join and participate in existing change initiatives. This might involve joining a departmental curriculum development

NEW DIRECTIONS FOR TEACHING AND LEARNING • DOI: 10.1002/tl

team or providing feedback to those developing plans or offering to pilot some of the recommended changes.

When there are no existing change initiatives, individuals can play the role of *cultivator,* fostering a climate to allow future change, by adapting the factors discussed previously. For example, the individual faculty member might develop a long-term vision for students in the program or become more informed about good practice in teaching the discipline or develop a scholarly interest in course development and instruction. The same faculty member might think more broadly about each of their own courses and, when designing or revising a course, speak to the instructors of courses that come before, during, and after to determine the skills, content, and attitudes being developed in the program. Discussion with these instructors will suggest areas of overlap and opportunities to build on existing knowledge and skill. The discussions may even open up questions about how students learn, as well as what they learn. The individual faculty member can seek out a consultant or mentor to help rethink a course and can invite a colleague to review and provide feedback on changes in a course. The more collegial the process, the better chance any changes will be positive and lasting, rather than ephemeral.

Looking Forward

Some of the departmental curriculum changes initiated under our Curriculum Innovation Grants are now five years old and are subject to all the forces to which university departments are usually subject, such as changes in personnel, enrollment growth, changes in university policy, and budget challenges. Our hope is that departments are different today as a result of these projects and that whatever curriculum results from the new environment will be guided by a new approach. This will become apparent in the processes used by departments and individuals as they engage in the next series of curriculum changes.

Curriculum change is a good mechanism for encouraging change in departmental culture. We think it a mistake to focus too much on the specifics of curriculum change in one department. Changes in students, institutional demands, and staff can quickly make specific changes in curriculum redundant. The more lasting change is a transformation in how a given department thinks about curriculum and teaching. Departmental consensus, a scholarly approach, and an emphasis on how students learn are key elements for an approach that results in lasting changes, well beyond the life of any specific project.

References

Barr, R., and Tagg, J. "From Teaching to Learning: A New Paradigm for Higher Education." *Change,* Nov.-Dec. 1995, pp. 13–25.
Biggs, J. *Teaching for Quality Learning at University.* Buckingham, U.K.: Society for Research in Higher Education and Open University Press, 1999.

Boyer Commission on Educating Undergraduates in the Research University. *Reinventing Undergraduate Education: A Blueprint for America's Research Universities.* Stony Brook, N.Y.: Boyer Commission on Educating Undergraduates in the Research University, 1998.

Bruner, J. S. *The Process of Education.* New York: Vintage, 1960.

Chickering, A., and Gamson, Z. "Seven Principles for Good Practice in Undergraduate Education." *American Association of Higher Education Bulletin,* 1987, *39*(7), 3–7.

Dickeson, R. C. *Prioritizing Academic Programs and Services: Reallocating Resources to Achieve a Strategic Balance.* San Francisco: Jossey-Bass, 1999.

Kotter, J. P. *Leading Change.* Boston: Harvard Business School Press, 1996.

Lindquist, J. *Strategies for Change.* Berkeley, Calif.: Pacific Soundings Press, 1978.

Posner, G. *Analyzing the Curriculum.* (3rd ed.) New York: McGraw-Hill, 2004.

Rogers, E. M., and Shoemaker, F. *Communication of Innovations: A Cross-Cultural Approach.* (2nd ed.) New York: Free Press, 1971.

Roy, D., "Weaving Inquiry into the First-Year Experience: A Rope of Sand." In C. Knapper (ed.), *Experiences with Inquiry Learning: Proceedings of a Symposium at McMaster University.* Hamilton, Ont.: Centre for Leadership in Learning, McMaster University, 2007.

Roy, D., and Day, R. *Active Learning Project.* Hamilton, Ont.: Centre for Leadership in Learning, McMaster University, 1999a. Retrieved May 16, 2007, from www.mcmaster.ca/cll/about.us/active.learning.project.htm.

Roy, D., and Day, R. *Imperial Oil Charitable Foundation: Departmental Learning Innovation Grants.* Hamilton, Ont.: Centre for Leadership in Learning, McMaster University, 1999b. Retrieved May 16, 2007, from www.mcmaster.ca/cll/money/learning.innovation.grants/index.htm.

Sell, G. R., and Lounsberry, B., "Supporting Curriculum Development." In J. G. Gaff, J. Ratcliff, and Associates (eds.), *Handbook of the Undergraduate Curriculum: A Comprehensive Guide to Purposes, Structures, Practices, and Change.* San Francisco: Jossey-Bass, 1997.

DALE ROY, PAOLA BORIN, *and* ERIKA KUSTRA *work in educational development in the Centre for Leadership in Learning, McMaster University, Ontario.*

NEW DIRECTIONS FOR TEACHING AND LEARNING • DOI: 10.1002/tl

4

This chapter describes the simple sustainable assessment protocols followed in food science at the University of Guelph to help ensure a continuously improving curriculum that satisfies the pedagogical prescriptions of the Institute of Food Technology, the learning objectives of the university, and learning outcomes of other stakeholders, including employers, students, and faculty.

Continuous Curriculum Assessment and Improvement: A Case Study

Art Hill

Many factors, including reduced teaching resources, higher student-to-teacher ratios, evolving teaching technologies, and increased emphasis on success skills, have made it necessary for many teaching faculties to become more deliberate about continuous curriculum assessment and improvement. An example is the evolution of food science education standards prescribed by the Institute of Food Technology (Hartel, 2001). The 1966 standards prescribed a food science knowledge base, the 1992 standards added requirements for statistics and success skills, and the 2001 standards prescribed outcome-based measures of learning, continuous curricular evaluation and improvement, and greater flexibility of curricular design. This chapter describes and reflects on the process followed in food science (FS) at the University of Guelph to help ensure a continuously improving curriculum that satisfies the pedagogical prescriptions of our external accreditation (by the Institute of Food Technology), the learning objectives of the university, and other stakeholders including employers, students, and faculty. A more general description of curriculum assessment based in part on the food science experience is available (Wolf, Hill, and Evers, 2006).

Critical insights and collaboration of Peter Wolf and Fred Evers, of Teaching Support Services, University of Guelph, are gratefully acknowledged. Many thanks also to food science students, teaching assistants, faculty, graduates, and employers for their roles in helping us become better educators of food scientists.

The foundational philosophy of the food science program is that teachers and teaching administrators should approach teaching as learners. To help us keep this principle in mind, we introduced the metaphorical learning fractal, a concept borrowed from physics that can be illustrated by a space traveler approaching the Vancouver shoreline. She first sees bays and peninsulas, then smaller bays and peninsulas within them, and then within those, still smaller bays and peninsulas, and so on. Such structures that appear similar at different scales are called fractals. Similarly, the fractal unit of learning is the experiential learning cycle (see Figure 4.1), which we understand as an approach to learning rather than a technique. Every learning activity, including the lowest level of knowledge acquisition (Anderson, Krathwohl, and Bloom, 2001), should require the learner to act, value, think, and decide (Kolb and Fry, 1975). In the context of curricular improvement, the learning fractal represents the application of experiential learning at all levels of development, delivery, and assessment.

Accordingly, this chapter describes the curricular improvement process at FS under headings that correspond to the elements of the dynamic model illustrated in Figure 4.1. To provide context for that discussion, we begin with a brief description of the food science program at Guelph.

Figure 4.1. The Learning Fractal Applied to Curricular Improvement

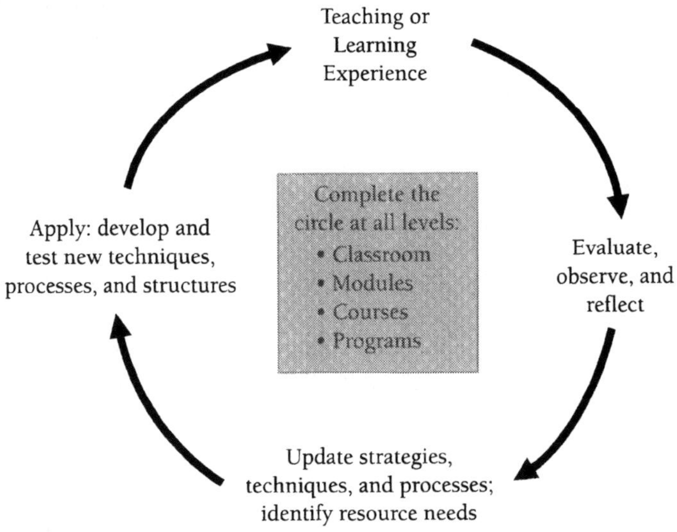

Source: Adapted from the learning circle of Kolb and Fry (1975).

Food Science at the University of Guelph

The Department of Food Science at Guelph is research-intensive, with a total of sixteen faculty, including six research chairs and about 100 graduate and 110 undergraduate students, of which more than 80 percent are women. Our program specifically allows students to prepare for research careers (graduate school) or professional careers or both. About 40 percent of our students take the coop option, which requires three fourteen-week work terms. We enjoy very close ties with the Ontario food industry, which is largely managed by our graduates, employs our coop students, provides numerous scholarships, and would happily employ many more than our annual output of about twenty-five graduates. Year 1 of the undergraduate program is BSc core courses. Year 2 completes the BSc core and includes three foundational courses in food science: (1) an introductory course establishes expectations for curricular applications of science to the study of food; (2) a communication course introduces various types of technical communications and establishes expectations for communication across the curriculum activities; and (3) a course in food engineering includes a numeracy guide and establishes curricular expectations in numeracy. The program is accredited by the Institute of Food Technology (Hartel, 2001).

Evaluate, Observe, and Reflect

Learning assessment in the FS more or less follows the four levels of the Kirkpatrick model for summative evaluation (Kirkpatrick and Kirkpatrick, 2006): namely, students' reaction, learning results, behavior in the workplace, and business results. For our purposes the levels were defined as follows:

Level 1. Students' reactions to the program: likes, dislikes, best learning experiences, relevance, and so forth.
Level 2. Learning results: achievement of learning objectives as assessed during and soon after the program.
Level 3. Behavior in the workplace and generally: in what ways and to what benefits are graduates applying the knowledge and skills learned at Guelph?
Level 4. Business results: in what ways has food science education helped employer organizations fulfill their missions or meet their objectives?

Four assessment tools are used. Student reactions (Level 1) are obtained via group exit interviews and postgraduate e-mail surveys. The short-term feedback from group exit interviews is especially helpful to identify strengths and weaknesses associated with new courses or new teaching strategies. We often make immediate changes based on these interviews. Learning results

(Level 2) are mainly assessed via individual student assessment. Behavior in the workplace and business results (Levels 3 and 4) are assessed by postgraduate e-mail surveys and employer interviews. These assessment tools and follow-up evaluation and reflection by professional teaching support staff and faculty and teaching assistants are summarized in Table 4.1.

Table 4.1. Summary of Assessment Tools

What, Who, When, and Levels	Questions or Issues Explored
What: In-course evaluation *Who:* Instructors and TAs *When:* Ongoing *Kirkpatrick levels:* 1, 2	Students' portfolios showing affective and skills development Traditional course-by-course individual assessment
What: Exit focus group *Who:* Graduating students *When:* Annual *Kirkpatrick levels:* 1, 2	Most enjoyable learning experiences Most important learning experiences What would you drop, add, or change?
What: Online survey *Who:* Recent grads, two to three years *When:* Triennial *Kirkpatrick levels:* 3, 4	Most significant learning experiences What aspects benefit you most in work and life? Your employer's mission? What would you drop, add, or change? What advice can you offer to first-year FS students?
What: Focus group lunch *Who:* Minimum five employers of FS grads *When:* Triennial *Kirkpatrick levels:* 3, 4	Do FS program content and learning objectives match your expectations for grads? Do you have other expectations? How well do our graduates meet them? Which FS training helps graduates meet your organization's goals? What advice can you offer to new FS grads?
What: External assessment *Who:* Institute of Food Technology *When:* Every five years *Kirkpatrick levels:* 2, 3, 4	Check off matrix used to assess LOs for all courses in five competency areas. Indicates participation in learning activities. Less useful for measuring learning outcomes.
What: Professional review *Who:* Teaching support staff *When:* Triennial *Kirkpatrick levels:* 2, 3, 4	University teaching support staff work with the department undergraduate committee to review all assessment data and prepare a SWOT-type review and analysis of the curriculum.
What: Half-day conference *Who:* Instructors and TAs *When:* Triennial *Kirkpatrick levels:* 2, 3, 4	Review all assessment data Complete SWOT analysis Suggests areas for improvement and strategies to explore and develop

Table 4.2. Learning Realms and Categories of Learning Objectives

Learning Realm	Subcategories	Comments
Knowledge and understanding	Historical Global Forms of inquiry Discipline	Balance science and academics versus technical and professional
Success skills	Communication Numeracy Technical, psychomotor	Learning outcomes are performance or product-based, so cross-curricular integration is vital
Affective	Self-awareness Moral maturity Independence of thought	Addressed in group projects, port-folios, and participative lectures

Update: Learning Objectives, Teaching Techniques, and Evaluation Techniques

The next step is to update cross-curricular and course-by-course learning objectives (LOs) and both teaching and evaluation techniques. The structures and processes we use to do that will probably evolve as we gain experience in effecting this continuous improvement model. Note that fall 2005 marked the completion of the first full cycle illustrated in Figure 4.1 and the beginning of the next. At the current time, LOs are grouped in learning realms (Table 4.2) and are informed by base competencies as described by Evers (1998), learning objectives of the university (University of Guelph, 2006), external accreditation standards, and, of course, the most recent program assessment. For examples, consider the following cross-curricular communications (numbers 1 and 2) and affective (numbers 3 and 4) LOs:

1. Write abstracts that succinctly and accurately summarize a scientific research project or the literature on a scientific topic
2. Give oral presentations that accurately communicate scientific information and hold the attention of the audience
3. Explain the elements of utilitarian and deontological ethics and accurately use moral terms such as ethics and values
4. Intelligently discuss controversial food-related issues such as genetically modified foods, nutritional labeling, and food security

Intelligent and dynamic cross-curricular distribution of learning activities, along with associated teaching and evaluation techniques (Figure 4.2), is achieved with the following tools:

Figure 4.2. A Matrix of Learning Objectives and Teaching Techniques for the Food Science Undergraduate Program

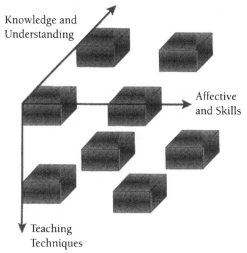

- A triennial faculty survey. Faculty are given a list of LOs and asked to answer the following questions for each course they are responsible for: Does this course contribute to this LO? If so, What teaching strategies are used to meet this LO? And, how is the LO outcome measured and evaluated? The result is a table that summarizes teaching strategies and learning objectives and outcomes for each course. A second shorter table summarizes curricular LO for each year in the program and cross-links them with courses and learning activities. Together these tables serve as a curricular map.
- A third table that cross-links course by course LO with lists of core competencies specified by our external accreditation body, the Institute of Food Technology.
- A summary of communication skills and a summary of numeracy skills cross-linked with corresponding cross-curricular learning activities.
- Detailed but generalized grading rubrics for written and oral presentations that help inform students and instructors about communication standards, although they are not used for all written and oral assignments.
- A cross-curricular numeracy guide that makes both students and instructors aware of the standards for numeracy in our program and provides supplementary training material to help students meet them.

All of this material is made available to faculty and students, but is probably little read except when attention is specifically drawn to it. That happens for faculty during triennial reviews. It happens for students in a second-year engineering course, which introduces the numeracy guide and

NEW DIRECTIONS FOR TEACHING AND LEARNING • DOI: 10.1002/tl

sets the bar for numeracy standards for the curriculum and, further, in a second-year communication course when curricular LOs are discussed and students are required to draft an online skills portfolio that is updated in a fourth-year course.

The update process concludes by integrating all this material into a brief description of the ideal food science graduate. The current word picture of "supergrad" has four points and is accompanied by an animated image of superwoman. Superwoman seemed appropriate because she can represent the 80 percent of our students who are female and perhaps attract more men into our program. Following is what a supergrad looks like:

- Describes, explains, and applies basic sciences to all aspects of food, from gate to plate
- Demonstrates a broad range of success skills
- Demonstrates positive affective qualities
- Has a sense of vocation and seeks a career path to fill it
- Can develop and test new techniques, processes, and structures

The time line for the triennial curricular improvement cycle requires approximately one to four months for evaluation, five to eight months to update it, and nine to thirty-six months to apply it. However, the phases overlap. The application phase, in particular, is continuous because we do not stop teaching while we evaluate, and because changes and improvements have their own time lines. For example, implementation of the continuous improvement model described here is the result of a 2001 program assessment. That same assessment recommended several new courses, course deletions, and major course revisions that were applied for the first time with the current 2007 graduating class.

It is important to be deliberate about applying the learning fractal (shown in Figure 4.1) during the implementation process, so there is a continuous tweaking of the curriculum at all levels. In other words, the third-year review is about steering the ship, suggesting cross-curricular changes, insertion or deletion of content and skills, and the like. Continuous improvement during the application phase means that we pay attention to the directions set at the third-year review and we're deliberate about assessing outcomes and making adjustments course by course and lecture by lecture.

Some Reflections

Assessment of learning outcomes is guided by the Kirkpatrick model, based on conventional assessment of individual students, annual surveys of senior students, and triennial surveys of graduates, employers, and faculty. This process is simple and economical. Surveys of multiple stakeholders provide substantive depth and breadth to our reflections on program quality. The surveys also enhance our relationships with stakeholders. In particular,

NEW DIRECTIONS FOR TEACHING AND LEARNING • DOI: 10.1002/tl

industry partners were pleased that their views were considered and applied. On the negative side, this assessment process is qualitative only, although it's not clear how much benefit would result from more costly quantitative surveys. For example, a quantitative survey (Clark, McCurdy, Roy, and Smith, 2006) of thirty-two recent graduates and twelve employers to assess the joint food science curriculum of Washington State University and University of Idaho concluded that students needed more training in food safety. Similarly, although our focus group of six employers rated our students highly for technical competence, they did suggest that Guelph food science graduates needed more training in food safety control systems. It seems likely that this common conclusion by two sets of employers reflects increasing concern of employers about food safety, rather than a real difference in technical competence of students with respect to food safety versus other areas of food science. Of course, this information is still valuable and tells us in effect that employers expect more competence in food safety than in other areas. We are now addressing that concern with enhanced cross-curricular modules on food safety and a new distance education course in food safety systems, which will provide accessible food safety training for current degree students and for graduates already working in the industry.

Continuous curricular improvement is visualized as a learning fractal (see Figure 4.1), which is foundational to all levels of learning and curricular development and assessment. The upward learning spiral ends and begins with a triennial conference where instructors, teaching assistants, student representatives, and professional teaching support staff use a strength, weakness, opportunities, and threats chart (SWOT) format to analyze assessment results and suggest curricular improvements. LOs are summarized with a word picture of a food science "supergrad" matched with diverse teaching and evaluation techniques and strategically placed across the curriculum to accommodate different learning styles. This group process is probably the most valuable component of the continuous improvement cycle. The most obvious benefits follow.

- Serious integration of knowledge-based content, skills training, and teaching techniques result, as faculty see what's happening in other courses and discuss strategies to synergize.
- The bars for innovation and teaching effectiveness are raised.
- The perceived value of teaching is increased.

In other words, the interactive nature of the process encourages instructors and teaching assistants to pay more attention to pedagogy, to explore how to teach better as well as what to teach. It some cases, it's not about exploring new techniques, but motivation to make obviously needed improvements.

Again, the qualitative nature of the assessment process means that the "concrete" evidence of these benefits is anecdotal rather than statistical. For example, comments made in exit interviews suggest that communicating across the curriculum, with respect to time invested by students and instructors, efficiently builds proficiency in communicating science to diverse audiences and also helps students achieve knowledge-based LOs. Students perceive that the requirement to communicate science to nonscientific audiences improves their communication skills and their understanding of the science. In practice this means, for example, that many traditional lab reports are replaced by alternative reporting formats such as technical reports, executive summaries, scientific abstracts, or even news releases.

Other tangible evidence of improved learning outcomes is that credited independent learning opportunities have increased despite static levels of base funding for our undergraduate program. These include summer research internships, more independent and team projects such as comprehensive product development projects, and communication or service projects. One student wrote a monthly column on food issues in the campus newspaper. Others have prepared and delivered training modules on food science for primary and secondary school science classes. Another developed a generic presentation on food science and various associated materials in support of a food science ambassador program sponsored by the Canadian Institute of Food Science. In a current project one of our students is working with a nutritionist and agencies external to the university to develop a training program in food choices and preparation to help seniors adapting to new life situations ensure that they get adequate nutrition using foods they enjoy. In other words, students are applying food science knowledge in real-world situations and achieving long-term benefits for the people they serve.

Portfolios. One challenge with portfolios is the lack of time available to orient students to the language of self-assessment, so providing a detailed and descriptive template is vital. The template used in our program was created by Evers (2005). After reading through the first completed set of portfolios from the 2007 graduating class, we find that the most important of all the portfolio assignments should be cross-curricular. The process in fourth year of upgrading a portfolio created in second year readily highlights progress made in all learning realms. The portfolio elements that seemed most important with respect to self-assessment, awareness, developing future goals, and a sense of vocation were the intellectual biography and the mission statement.

Sustainability. Finally, it is important to reflect on the robustness or sustainability of continuous curriculum improvement. The food science curricular improvement protocol, as illustrated in Figure 4.3, is based on the learning fractal and is focused on clear learning outcomes, accountable to stakeholders, simple, flexible, incremental, resourced, and championed. These properties are essential to ensure sustainability.

- The learning fractal establishes a philosophical foundation. It is a constant reminder to complete the learning circle at every level of course and curricular development and improvement.

NEW DIRECTIONS FOR TEACHING AND LEARNING • DOI: 10.1002/tl

Figure 4.3. Operating Principles of Effective and Continuous Curriculum Improvement

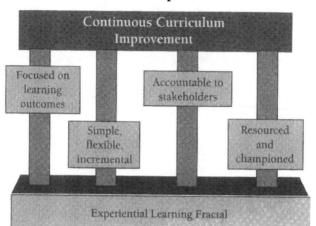

- Development of learning outcomes in consultation with stakeholders ensures communication and accountability. For example, our first review of LOs and teaching strategies (in 2003) recommended that food science instructors consult with instructors in first- and second-year science courses to set knowledge standards in our follow-up courses (most of our specialized program begins in the third semester after base science courses are completed). One professor did that consultation and described favorable outcomes at a subsequent teaching conference, with the result that other faculty went away intending to do the same. This illustrates the importance of group process to motivate instructors to make obvious improvements in their own courses and cooperate with curricular improvements. Positive responses from graduates and employers also motivate instructors to innovate and communicate about teaching.
- Simple and flexible surveys of stakeholders (as opposed to more detailed and quantitative surveys) help and motivate instructors to identify problems and solutions without onerous protocols. Implementation strategies also need to be flexible and incremental. Patient and incremental application allows time for instructor buy-in and for feedback and corrections during implementation. Instructors need room to apply, or sometimes not to apply, recommended changes in their own way. Curriculum committees need to encourage and direct, but as much as possible to avoid prescriptions. Pedagogical mandates from on high are rarely well received by the instructors expected to implement them.

NEW DIRECTIONS FOR TEACHING AND LEARNING • DOI: 10.1002/tl

The fourth pillar supporting continuous curriculum improvement, as shown in Figure 4.3, is resources and leadership. As we moved from casual and irregular course and curriculum assessment to more deliberate protocols, it became necessary to champion the process from within the department and obtain expert support from outside the department. Teaching support professionals helped plan assessment protocols and design surveys, facilitated focus groups and teaching conferences, and helped analyze the assessment results and build recommendations. These collaborations with teaching support staff provide both encouragement and accountability for champions within the department. Administrative support at department and college levels is also critical to ensure resources and help embed curriculum assessment and improvement into the department culture, so that it will survive after the current champion(s) moves on.

Transferability. I hesitate to comment on the likely success of applying the protocols described in this paper to other types of undergraduate programs. However, I think the properties of effective and continuous curriculum improvement described here (Figure 4.3) are in principle transferable to any program, provided that unique properties of each program are considered and accounted for. For example, our program enjoys the benefit of close ties with the food industry, while other programs may lack opportunity to build rapport with employer stakeholders. So with respect to the Kirkpatrick assessment levels described above, it may be impractical for some programs to do Level 4 assessment, but any program could benefit from assessment at Levels 1 and 2 and, with some adjustment of wording, from Level 3. Kirkpatrick and others may not agree, but in my view Level 3 assessment is based on the premise that learning is not its own end, so it is important to understand how the undergraduate experience is affecting the lives of graduates and through them the world in which they live. The process and the outcomes of preparing and executing quality assessment protocols to at least attempt to answer that question will benefit any teaching endeavor.

Next Steps

With reference to the learning fractal (shown in Figure 4.1), the history of this process at Guelph began with an informal assessment in 2001, including a teaching conference with participation by employers, and resulted in a recommendation to build a protocol for continual curriculum assessment and improvement. Many changes to the curriculum and individual course content and teaching strategies were also recommended and implemented for the fall 2003 cohort. During winter and fall 2005 we completed the several assessments recommended in the 2001 review and are now continuing in the update and application phases (see Figure 4.1). So far so good, but some steps are needed to ensure continued momentum. Suggested next steps include:

NEW DIRECTIONS FOR TEACHING AND LEARNING • DOI: 10.1002/tl

1. Simplify the reporting formats. The processes are simple, but we still generate a lot of paper, partly because we report some data in multiple formats so as to be better prepared for reviews by internal and external accrediting agencies.
2. Hold more frequent teaching conferences for our own faculty and teaching assistants. In fall 2006 we held a three-hour teaching conference to follow up recommendations from the fall 2005 triennial review and conference. It is evident that we need a three-hour teaching conference facilitated by teaching professionals external to the department at least once a year in addition to online postings and occasional updates at faculty meetings.
3. The triennial review will include an evaluation of the assessment and improvement process.
4. As with this chapter and similar communications, the process of reporting and receiving external feedback on what we are doing helps evolve the assessment protocols and creates a sense of accountability.

Conclusion

This chapter is about continuous curriculum improvement. This topic could be taken negatively, as implying that what we are currently doing is deficient, or be taken presumptuously, as implying that proposed changes are always for the better. Alternative wording for this topic is continuous curriculum optimization, meaning that we need to continuously optimize what we teach and how we teach it for changes in culture, teaching technologies, teaching staff, stakeholder interests, resources, and so forth. The simple and flexible assessment and curriculum revision protocols that we are following in food science provide essential information and an environment of communication among all stakeholders to help us adapt to changing conditions and continuously optimize teaching strategies, techniques, content, and resources. An added bonus is that we will always be ready for internal (university-mandated) and external (in our case, the Institute of Food Technology) reviews, which happen at irregular intervals.

References

Anderson, L., Krathwohl, D., and Bloom, B. *Taxonomy for Learning, Teaching, and Assessing: A Revision of Bloom's Taxonomy of Educational Objectives.* New York: Longman, 2001.
Clark, S., McCurdy, S., Roy, S., and Smith, D. "Assessment of the Joint Food Science Curriculum of Washington State University and the University of Idaho by Graduates and Their Employees." *Journal of Food Science Education,* 2006, 1, 9–14.
Department of Food Science, University of Guelph. "Undergraduate Program Assessment and Development Advisory." 2007.
Evers, F. *The Bases of Competency: Skills for Lifelong Learning and Employability.* San Francisco: Jossey-Bass, 1998.

Evers, F. "Bases of Competencies Skills Portfolio Specifications." 2005. Retrieved May 20, 2007, from www.uoguelph.ca/cera/PDFs.

Hartel, R. "IFT Revises Its Education Standards." *Food Technology*, 2001, *55*, 53.

Kirkpatrick, D., and Kirkpatrick, J. *Evaluating Training Programs: The Four Levels.* (3rd ed.) San Francisco: Berrett-Koehler, 2006.

Kolb, D. A., and Fry, R. "Toward an Applied Theory of Experiential Learning." In C. Cooper (ed.), *Theories of Group Processes.* London: Wiley, 1975.

University of Guelph. "Learning Objectives: 2006–2007 Undergraduate Calendar." 2006.

Wolf, P., Hill, A., Evers, F. *Handbook for Curriculum Assessment.* Hamilton, Ont.: Educational Research and Development Unit, University of Guelph, 2006.

ART HILL is associate professor in the Department of Food Science at the University of Guelph.

NEW DIRECTIONS FOR TEACHING AND LEARNING • DOI: 10.1002/tl

5

This chapter describes the development of a new major in Adult Development, Families, and Well-Being in the Department of Family Relations and Applied Nutrition.

Designing a New Program in Family Relations and Applied Nutrition

Sharon Mayne Devine, Kerry Daly, Donna Lero,
Clare MacMartin

The Department of Family Relations and Applied Nutrition is located in a 105-year-old building; a walk around the building reveals the various renovation and restoration projects that have occurred over the years. We are proud of our old building, and in many ways it tells the story of our department. This chapter is a description of the first phase of one of our many restoration and renovation projects, the development of a new major in Adult Development, Families, and Well-Being (ADFW), to be offered in the fall of 2007.

Mobilizing for Change

Family Relations and Applied Nutrition is an interdisciplinary department that offered three undergraduate majors: child, youth, and family (CYF); applied human nutrition; and gerontology; as well as graduate programs at the master's and doctoral levels. Several factors precipitated a review of the gerontology major and thoughts about designing a new major. One was declining enrollments in our gerontology program, which we learned is a common phenomenon across North America. We had removed our undergraduate family and social relations major several years prior and were

We are pleased to acknowledge the other members of the Working Group: Scott Maitland, Michelle Preyde, Carolyn Tubbs, and Linda Zehr.

looking for a way to include our continuing strengths in family relationships and processes. Furthermore, we had two faculty vacancies that required us to articulate a longer-term recruitment plan. Externally, we had partnered with another institution to deliver programs in early childhood services and in family and community social services. Our challenge was to create a new major that capitalized on our established strengths and would position the new major without overlapping with our other offerings. After a number of unsuccessful attempts to modify the gerontology major to be more attractive to students, we were given the message by the dean that a more fundamental change was required. Although it seemed ludicrous to drop the gerontology major at a time when the population is aging, the writing was on the wall.

Experiencing the problem without direction. To see "writing on the wall" is an insufficient catalyst for organizational change. One of our first and perhaps most significant challenges in the department was to move from an awareness of the need for change to an open and collective naming of the problem and a decision to make a change. We first had to work our way through a number of efforts to keep things as they were with minor modifications. During these early stages, there was no consensus and conversations were often awkward and stilted due to different interests, stakes, and investments in the major. These discussions were difficult for many people in the department because they raised uncertainty about future roles, questions of loyalty and allegiance, and arguments about the effects of this change on alumni, community partnerships, and reputation. At this time there was a reluctance to simply drop the major without knowing what would take its place.

Cultivating a commitment for change. Although it seemed that we floundered without direction at these early stages, these were necessary discussions (in retrospect) in order to at least embrace the idea that the status quo was no longer viable. Pressure from the administration, growing conflict within the department, and the time pressure associated with an impending admission cycle deepened our collective awareness that change was necessary. It was as if we needed to deepen our awareness of the crisis at hand in order to fortify our resolve to make a difficult change.

Opening space to consider alternatives. In order to get unstuck, we designed a two-day strategic planning exercise that would provide an opportunity for thinking through a set of options. Through a series of roundtable, "blue-sky" discussions that included all faculty and staff, we endeavored to clarify our identity and mission as a department, identify our strengths, and imagine future possibilities. In this process we took into account market forces, internal resources, and emerging needs for professional education in our areas of strength. At the end of two days, we had identified some future directions and set up working groups to develop these ideas. Through a number of separate roundtable discussions, faculty and staff had further opportunities to identify current limitations of the gerontology major, growing constraints on resources in trying to service a small number of students,

NEW DIRECTIONS FOR TEACHING AND LEARNING • DOI: 10.1002/tl

and opportunity costs associated with forgoing other possibilities. Furthermore, the process provided an opportunity to look at the full spectrum of programs we delivered and to consider how something new might fit within the larger context of our departmental mission. As new possibilities emerged, we gained clarity about the limitations of the current major. Our next step was to form a small working group with Sharon and Donna as leaders to develop a proposal for the new major.

Facilitating Curriculum Development

We realized that people in the department were ready for change, and we also knew that it was necessary and that it had to happen quickly. We had a very tight time line in which to accomplish our task, because particular dates for approvals through various committees had to be met for the new major to be included in the university calendar and students to be admitted the following academic year. We were also confronted with the fact that if we did not accomplish our task, the gerontology major would stay in the university calendar for one more year and we would have to admit another year of a small cohort of students into the program. Although the time lines were extremely tight, the department supported the working group to meet these deadlines. In retrospect this sense of urgency was useful because it galvanized the department, helping to keep us focused, open, and on task.

We did not see the point we had reached—needing to reinvent ourselves—as a point of failure. In our view it created an opportunity to rebuild, renew, and revitalize our joint efforts. In fact, some saw it as a critically important opportunity to reconnect our program offerings with the core strengths of our faculty and to provide us with some fresh perspective on the contributions our department could make in undergraduate education and to the training of professionals in a variety of human services. All faculty wanted to see a positive, creative resolution to our "problem" that could provide new opportunities for us as faculty, be attractive to a range of students, and retain our reputation for academic excellence and innovation.

Creating a Vision. As a working group, we began by creating a vision that would guide us in developing the new major and identifying important steps and processes to reach that goal. First we gathered materials from the strategic planning process in order to capture the ideas generated by the department. One of those ideas included our awareness of the need for and value of an interdisciplinary program that provides broad knowledge about individual development and family relationships across the life span. Second we conducted a review of university web sites of departments and majors across North America that we considered benchmarks of excellence. We next conducted a survey of existing students in the department to discover what they identified as our strengths and weaknesses. We also developed an appreciation of the diversity of career opportunities that could be served by the new major through contacts

NEW DIRECTIONS FOR TEACHING AND LEARNING • DOI: 10.1002/tl

with community partners, policymakers, research funders, and community service planners, as well as by identifying occupations and career paths that had been selected by graduates of the department in recent years.

From this information we generated our vision for an exciting interdisciplinary program with a core knowledge base that could provide a home for students with particular interests in adulthood and aging and would also be attractive to students with interests in human sexuality, family relationships, and social policy. The new major would be designed for students with career goals of working in parent and family support programs; in work with seniors, caregivers, and agencies that address their needs; or in sexuality education, counseling, social work, and program development in the social service sector; as well as those who might undertake research, policy development, or teaching in related areas.

In Need of a Map. Once we had our vision we needed to craft the major. We identified a need for a map to help us navigate through the complexity of the task. At this point we contacted the curriculum design consultant at Teaching Support Services (Peter Wolf) and reviewed with him what we had already accomplished. The consultant raised an important question: How do you know there is a need for this program? We believed that there was. The consultant identified two approaches to developing a new major: (1) build it and they will come or (2) create a program in response to an identified community need. We were in effect doing both, taking a hybrid approach. We were working creatively with the tension between who we were as a department (our history, knowledge, expertise, and research interests), the need for renewal, and a desire and commitment to be responsive to the community we serve.

The consultant shared with us a comprehensive model of curriculum evolution (Wolf, 2006) that included three distinct components: curriculum visioning, curriculum development, and course coordination and development. Because of our strict time line, we were not able to go through this process in the way it had been outlined. We already had a vision, had begun a process of gathering information from students and community agencies, and had courses "on the books" that we felt could be appropriate for the major. Together we engaged in a messy, hybrid process with the tools, resources, and appropriate questions to challenge us.

Designing the New Major: Creating Possibilities

We started by identifying knowledge domains that included introductory foundation courses in the social and biological sciences; prescribed courses in our department from three thematic content areas (developmental and aging perspectives, family and social relationships, and health and well-being); and courses that met our criteria for providing knowledge about research methods and developing professional practice skills. Beyond that step, we identified courses in our department and others that would be

NEW DIRECTIONS FOR TEACHING AND LEARNING • DOI: 10.1002/tl

identified as relevant to students with particular interests in the three thematic content areas. These would be listed in the calendar as courses students could select to deepen their knowledge or to prepare for a particular career, but not listed as required courses for specializations. Offering more electives would also serve the purposes of students who plan to go on to a faculty of education, since most of these require that students have several electives and/or a second "teachable" subject. We successfully struggled with the tension between wanting to include more required courses in the major and our goal of providing flexible options for students with diverse interests. As part of this consideration, we designed the major with room for students to take a minor in areas such as public administration, business, or women's studies and committed ourselves to develop a co-op option for students to obtain paid work experience as part of their program. We also recognized that by providing options for students, we were requiring them to make choices and take more responsibility for their learning.

Through this process we developed a working description of the new major that included options for minors incorporating both topical streams (such as family relations and adulthood, and aging) and directional streams (applied service, or applied research or academic streams). The major would focus on human development across the life span, with a particular emphasis on adulthood. There would be three focal points of the major: human development and aging, family and social relations across the life span, and determinants of health and well-being. Core courses could include a strong focus on individual development and social relationships across the life span, work and family issues, human sexuality, diversity among individuals and families, and adulthood and aging. Course work on policies, services, and family and community contexts that affect individual and family health and well-being and at least one placement course in a community agency provide additional knowledge and skills. See the appendix at the end of this chapter for the calendar description of the new major.

Once we had solidified this description of the new major, we began the process of articulating the attributes of the ideal graduate to help us develop our program objectives and a description of core competencies. We set up a half-day workshop and divided faculty into three working groups. Faculty identified the ideal attributes of a graduate of this new major along three dimensions: core values, skills and competencies, and knowledge domains. These were some of the most dynamic discussions we had throughout the entire process and resulted in the development of the attributes of the ideal graduate (see Exhibit 5.1).

Our next task was to hold two focus groups: one with our community partners and another with undergraduate students in the department. At all of these meetings we presented the description of the new major and our list of attributes. We sought input on important program components, from their perspective, and discussed experiential learning opportunities,

Exhibit 5.1. Attributes of the Ideal Graduate

Core Values	Skills and Competencies	Knowledge Domains
Individual and interpersonal • Compassion, empathy • Sensitivity to diversity • Initiative, self-direction, and creativity • Belief in lifelong learning • Flexibility and adaptability • Awareness of personal boundaries *Organizational* • Team player • Facilitator • Effective communicator *Professional and ethical* • Professional, ethical, and confidential conduct • Appropriate appearance, dress, and deportment • Knowledge-based competence *Political* • Social justice, social accountability • Active citizenship via service, community engagement • Politically aware, globally aware	*Clinical* • Assessment • Counseling • Working with groups • Interpersonal communication • Conflict resolution and problem solving *Administrative* • Planning and organizing time management • Strategic thinking • Program development, implementation, and evaluation • Fundraising and public relations *Community engagement* • Social policies • Understanding and navigating through community services, agencies, and nonprofits • Social advocacy *Research* • Critical thinking • Awareness of social and economic determinants of health, multiculturalism, and family systems, dynamics, and patterns • Research-service synthesis using evidence-based practice	*Orienting subject matter* • Lifespan and human development • Sociology • Psychology • Physiology *Thematic content areas* • Developmental and aging perspectives: intergenerational issues, sexual development, and theories of development • Family and social relationships: family diversity, parenting issues, and family theory • Health and well-being: nutrition, sexuality, determinants of health, culture and diversity, social policies, aging, work-life balance, and mental health *Practice-research stream* • Preparation for professional practice: communication and counseling, group work, professional issues and ethics, assessment, program design, administration, and community development and capacity building • Research stream: methods, statistics, and thesis

marketability, and desired skills and competencies. In all of these discussions, the new major proposal was well received.

The Weaving Process. To accomplish all of these tasks, the working group engaged in ongoing consultations with members of the department. Like architects, our process entailed developing proposals, presenting our ideas to the faculty and other stakeholders, incorporating feedback, making modifications, and then returning to the department for further feedback. In this way the members of the department owned the new major. We broke out of our traditional format for departmental meetings. To create something

NEW DIRECTIONS FOR TEACHING AND LEARNING • DOI: 10.1002/tl

innovative, we needed an innovative process. We broke into small groups, posted questions for discussion, and recorded input on flip chart paper. This approach maximized faculty input. Throughout this process, there was constructive and creative feedback as well as reemerging resistance to the proposed changes.

What's in a Name? It is important to underscore that one of the most difficult challenges we faced throughout this process was agreeing on a name for our new major. The name reflects identity, purpose, and ultimately is critical for shaping how we are seen by students, parents, guidance counselors, governments, and employers. The working group brought various options for names to the department and, of course, members of the department suggested others. We narrowed the choices and presented them to our community partners. We wanted to convey that our focus encompasses adulthood and aging, health, and family relationships. It was only when we were up against our submission deadline that faculty finally agreed on *adult development, families, and well-being*. This felt like a capstone decision after such an intensive process.

What We Have Learned: Internal Perspectives

When reflecting on the process of developing the new major, we identified a number of important lessons, most of which reflected points of tension or competing pressures. One lesson was to recognize and accept the tensions between a progress-oriented desire to push the activities of curriculum design forward and a process-oriented wish to pull back in order to listen to and incorporate the contributions of others. Most fruitful was adopting a deliberately nondefensive stance to avoid power struggles as they emerged.

Similarly, we recognized the importance of paying close attention to external influences while building on our unique strengths, values, and experience. To understand external influences and gain new perspective, we deliberately benchmarked the development of the ADFW major in relation to similar programs distinguished by their excellence in other universities. An orientation to the perspectives of external stakeholders, including partners in government, community placement partners, prospective employers of ADFW graduates, and high school students and guidance counselors, was also critical.

Timing was an additional source of tension. It was important to move activities forward in accordance with time lines laid out in a clear plan emerging from (and consistent with) the departmental strategic planning exercise. We also recognized the tension that exists in any initiative between plans to meet the interests of the few versus those of the collective.

We all learned the value of choosing facilitation from outside the department, once the decision had been made to launch the ADFW major. The consultant was able to engage people effectively in a trust-building process so that any decisions made served the collective good of the department and gave priority to optimizing student learning in the new major. The use of neutral leadership, expertise, and facilitation from outside the department, without a stake in the outcome, allowed department members the opportunity to open new ground or ask difficult and uncomfortable questions.

Links to the literature. One of the benefits of reflecting on the process we went through is the opportunity to stand back and see more clearly the strategies that were effective, the tensions that emerged, and the challenges we encountered. It also gave us an opportunity to consider what we might learn from the process in relation to existing literature on leading academic change. At the outset of the process, we did not follow an established model of change; we were preoccupied with the complexity of the crisis and, like most faculty, we were not models of curriculum change. Our opportunity to reflect on the process now has taken us to some of the existing literature on leading curriculum change. In examining this material, we are aware that in some ways we were successful in reinventing the wheel without the benefit of existing blueprints! Piecing together what we learned through experience and what we learned from existing literature, we highlight the following as critical elements in the process.

Cultivating a climate for change. One of the critical elements in mobilizing our change efforts was the importance of "establishing a sense of urgency" (Kotter, 1996, p. 35). Although there was awareness in our department of the need to change the existing gerontology major, it was not until we encountered the "perfect storm" that included high levels of external pressure, increasing awareness of internal consequences, and time pressures brought on by related decisions (such as faculty replacement) that we had to act. At this stage, our most important task was to name and embrace the crisis before us and to communicate to department members the urgency for making change.

Recognizing and managing competing interests. Dramatic change to the curriculum can bring to the fore both supporters of change and protectors of the status quo (Ferren and Mussell, 2000). Indeed, resistance to any proposed change is both natural and expected (Lucas, 2000). In our experience, current students were both receptive to changing what they had identified as problematic aspects of the curriculum and reluctant to lose the current major that they had identified with and invested in. Furthermore, established curricula are often characterized by faculty ownership of individual pieces of the curriculum (Graff, 1988), which can create tensions between individual stakes and the collective recognized need for change. Managing various constituencies and competing interests required open and transparent communication, multiple opportunities for input, and at times external facilitation to help us stay focused on the big picture.

Articulating the longer-term vision in which change will occur. Strategic planning in an academic setting is a means by which units can take an active role in shaping their future history by articulating their values and strengths, analyzing threats and opportunities in changing market conditions, and examining their competitive position based on an assessment of their strengths (Keller, 1983). Our strategic planning process provided the opportunity to discuss our values and strengths and to propose creative ideas that could move us in new directions. Furthermore, this process involves not just rational planning but "political maneuvering" and "psychology interplay" (Keller, 1983, p. 148). In the process we went through it was necessary to work through discussions that were both "participatory and highly tolerant of controversy" (p. 148).

Identifying and mobilizing leaders and empowering action. While broad participation is necessary when formulating a strategic vision, taking action to realize that vision is contingent on a guiding coalition of leaders and team players who have the power to lead the change (Kotter, 1996). Many kinds of leaders were needed in our effort to change the major, including administrators, cochairs of the working group, and external facilitators. Furthermore, the working group itself played a leadership role by staying on task and persistently moving forward through a series of difficult decisions and challenges. An important component of ensuring their continued progress was to empower the members of the group to boldly and creatively move toward the vision. In addition, these leaders had to be supported by administration with help in removing obstacles, changing structures that can undermine the vision, and encouraging risk-taking activities and actions (Kotter, 1996).

Articulating time lines with achievable goals. One of the benefits of moving with a sense of urgency is that deadlines move the agenda forward in an expedient manner. There is little room for complacency when time lines set by external review committees must be met. Critical here, as Kotter (1996) has suggested, is achieving "short-term wins" along the way that can energize and reward the team players who are moving the change process forward. For example, in creating our new major we experienced wins by coming to a consensus on the required skills and competencies, receiving constructive and supportive feedback from community focus groups, and reaching agreement about the name of the new major. Each of these wins involved a process of engaged decision making and buy-in from various stakeholders (such as students, faculty, and community) that served to solidify support and build consensus.

Recognizing success, consolidating gains, and maintaining momentum. The final stage of the change process involves recognition and celebration of goals that have been met. It is also necessary to consolidate the gains made by ensuring that the required resources and support are provided to implement the change (for example, by hiring and developing people who can implement the change vision) (Kotter, 1996). Furthermore, in light of homeostatic forces that may still retreat toward prior structures, it is important to maintain momentum in the implementation of change (Kotter, 1996).

At times this process was difficult for the working group and for the larger department; times when it would have been easier to find a program at another university that we could just replicate; times in meetings when holding the tensions between change and no change were difficult. Nevertheless, we have learned a great deal about the practical and political challenges of curriculum change—learnings that we are using as we continue the work of reviewing our curriculum offerings in the department.

NEW DIRECTIONS FOR TEACHING AND LEARNING • DOI: 10.1002/tl

We are now ready to launch our new major. We have built it in consultation with students, faculty, and the community. Will they come? We wait to see.

Appendix: Calendar Material Describing the Adult Development, Families, and Well-Being Major

Department of Family Relations and Applied Nutrition, College of Social and Applied Human Sciences

The Adult Development, Families, and Well-Being major focuses on health and well-being from young adulthood to old age within the context of changing family relationships and diverse social and cultural influences. Courses focus on current research and theory in adult development and aging, family relationships, human sexuality, social policy, and community services. Field placements and community service learning opportunities enable students to gain knowledge, skills, and values appropriate for work with individuals and groups in a variety of settings.

Graduates of this program are pursuing careers in a variety of settings, including family and community service agencies, government departments, services for seniors and their families, health care agencies, employee and family assistance programs, and local social planning councils. This program provides a solid foundation for the pursuit of graduate studies in fields such as social work, family relations, gerontology, occupational therapy, family law and mediation, couple and family therapy, education, sexual health, human resource management (business), and health studies.

This interdisciplinary program is designed to provide students with an understanding of the influence of psychological, social, biological, and economic factors on individual development, capabilities, health, and relationships across the life span. It is one of several majors in the department that share an overriding goal of applying knowledge to promote individual and family well-being. This major offers a high degree of flexibility for students, who may choose to deepen their studies in one or more of the core content areas in the major (adulthood and aging, family and social relationships, human sexuality, or health and well-being) and/or to choose electives in a related or complementary field.

References

Ferren, A. S., and Mussell, K. "Leading Curriculum Renewal." In A. F. Lucas (ed.), *Leading Academic Change: Essential Roles for Department Chairs*. San Francisco: Jossey-Bass, 2000.

Graff, G. *Professing Literature: An Institutional History*. Chicago: University of Chicago Press, 1988.

Keller, G. *Academic Strategy: The Management Revolution in American Higher Education*. Baltimore: Johns Hopkins University Press, 1983.

Kotter, J. *Leading Change.* Boston: Harvard Business School Press, 1996.

Lucas, A. "A Collaborative Model for Leading Academic Change." In A. F. Lucas (ed.), *Leading Academic Change: Essential Roles for Department Chairs.* San Francisco: Jossey-Bass, 2000.

Wolf, P. *Curriculum Evolution.* Guelph, Ont.: University of Guelph, 2006.

SHARON MAYNE DEVINE is a lecturer in the Department of Family Relations and Applied Nutrition at the University of Guelph and cochair of the working group responsible for the development of the new major.

KERRY DALY is professor and chair in the Department of Family Relations and Applied Nutrition at the University of Guelph.

DONNA LERO is associate professor in the Department of Family Relations and Applied Nutrition at the University of Guelph and cochair of the working group responsible for the development of the new major.

CLARE MACMARTIN is associate professor and associate chair in the Department of Family Relations and Applied Nutrition at the University of Guelph.

NEW DIRECTIONS FOR TEACHING AND LEARNING • DOI: 10.1002/tl

This chapter describes how student- and faculty-driven
curriculum assessment has facilitated the stability and
coherence of a variable-content interdisciplinary program
core.

Between Cultures: Using Curriculum Assessment to Develop and Deliver the Integrated Core of an Arts and Sciences Program

Donna Palmateer Pennee

How do you develop and deliver the integrated core of a cross-disciplinary arts and sciences undergraduate degree when the degree program has no departmental or college home and no full-time faculty, but plenty of enthusiastic students who are looking for a unique educational experience? This chapter outlines how a formalized curriculum assessment process performed a crucial infrastructural role in the development and delivery of a program that falls not only between disciplinary cultures but between the traditional cultures of university administration of faculty assignment, faculty evaluation, and curriculum evolution.

Origins of the Program

In 1990, students entering the University of Guelph for a BA or BSc degree could choose to enroll in the Akademia program, a unique first-year experience in which, through topic- or theme-based courses, they were encouraged to integrate the perspectives of the arts, social sciences, and natural sciences. Students were both excited and disappointed by this first-year program: excited by the intellectual challenges and social relevance of their integrated courses—disappointed that the experience ended after the first

NEW DIRECTIONS FOR TEACHING AND LEARNING, no. 112, Winter 2007   © Wiley Periodicals, Inc.
Published online in Wiley InterScience (www.interscience.wiley.com) • DOI: 10.1002/tl.298

year and that the welcome opportunity for breadth and integration came with the cost of delayed access to disciplinary degree requirements and a longer time to completion. Their disappointment taught program developers a valuable lesson—namely, that new curricular opportunities such as Akade-mia must be more than a supplement to the same old degree requirements: you need to rethink the whole venture. Two steering committees later, Akademia was discontinued in order to usher in the baccalaureate in arts and sciences (BAS). Students for whom Akademia had provided just a taste of the possibilities of integrating rather than polarizing "two cultures" now had access to a four-year program that would, in theory, better satisfy their intellectual and civic appetites.

Students continue to be the ones who drive this program, because they know firsthand and are most articulate about the program's strengths and weaknesses. After all, they know they are looking for something other than the increasingly specialized disciplinary route to BSc and BA training for graduate school, professional programs, or other worlds of work. They have given up the more traditional and easily recognized major in favor of a program that comprises a BSc minor, a BA minor, and an arts and sciences (ASCI) core open only to BAS students. At just 3.00 of 20.00 credits in this honors (or four-year) degree, the ASCI core is the value-added component that must make all the compensatory difference for students who do not have (or want) a ready answer to the question frequently asked of them, "Yes, but what's your major?"

Infrastructural Cultures and the Culture of Curriculum Development

The administrative and fiscal structures of universities are, alas, not as flexible as the students who select this degree. Disciplines and faculty, budgets and policies, and cultures of communication and practice tend to be housed and funded in college and departmental envelopes. The ASCI core, like the BAS program that it defines, has no disciplinary, departmental, or college home, no faculty whose time is fully dedicated to it, no sanctioned course evaluation form unique to its integrative goals, no departmental chair or performance review committee to assess the particular quality of the design and delivery of ASCI courses by faculty assigned from different disciplinary, departmental, and college homes. The BAS as approved by senate (in 2000) represented a structure built largely from ingredients already provided by the B.A. and B.Sc. programs (seventeen out of twenty credits), with a visionary but in effect virtual three-credit core that was to integrate the disciplinary silos of the "two cultures." Many questions arising from the logistics of the development and delivery of the ASCI core were left outside of the proposal. Beyond suitably generic course titles (for flexibility in staffing), answering the questions of how the ASCI content would be filled in, by which faculty members, and with what disciplinary affiliations was always an open-ended process.

NEW DIRECTIONS FOR TEACHING AND LEARNING • DOI: 10.1002/tl

Working on the BAS core permitted curricular issues to come into sharp relief as also infrastructural issues in ways that are often invisible to more traditional program and departmental cultures. So-called interdisciplinary programs—some of them real academic experiments, others short-sighted responses to fiscal crises—usually depend on a combination of items from a menu of courses and degree requirements that already exist, in a structure that leaves it up to the students to do the work of integrating the in-between. The BAS expressly seeks to provide core degree requirements that would foster these in-between habits of mind and not leave them to chance—but the curricular quality, stability, and coherence of this in-between core in effect was left to chance because of its location (but nonfit) amidst the pressures of departmental accountability, disciplinary traditions, systemic practices, and other manifestations of institutional cultural incompatibilities. That's where curriculum assessment became a crucial tool, used as a formative, if you will, rather than summative (or simply periodic) evaluation of a program's success.

When only three out of twenty credits constitute the uniqueness of the program (in combination with required minors from usually disparate cultures), what is "the curriculum" that needs to evolve, and who is to do the work of making the vision a reality? How would we develop the ASCI curriculum in conscious and shared ways when BAS program committee members and ASCI instructors are not members of a single administrative unit or disciplinary culture? How could we be sure that individual ASCI courses were really "BAS" courses, that faculty delivering them were really committed to making them ASCI courses and not simply teaching (for example) a philosophy course (if taught by a philosopher), or a history course (if taught by a historian)? How could we be sure that ASCI teaching would not be treated by a department chair as a waste of precious departmental resources? How could we be sure that the students would not be treated as "failed" scientists (if taught in an ASCI course by a chemist or a physicist for whom disciplinary specificity drove the pedagogy and evaluation)? Co- or team-teaching seems like the obvious answer, but it multiplies the concerns involved in finding even one faculty member per course: time to get the right team together, time to let them collaborate on course development, energy to calibrate (and resources to give) credit for teaching in increments smaller than the typical course in a less than typical degree program, and so on.

Disciplinary barriers, particularly perception of differences in difficulty of subject matter, could affect a dean's or chair's choice of who to assign to an ASCI course, but also a performance committee's perceptions of the worth of teaching outside one's own unit in a program such as the BAS. At performance and evaluation time, ASCI teaching will be evaluated by people who may know little or nothing about the BAS program; standardized (departmental or college) evaluation forms limit the kinds of information that can be collected about this specific program's improvement; and the efficacy of the feedback is limited when it remains confidential to the disciplinary space

NEW DIRECTIONS FOR TEACHING AND LEARNING • DOI: 10.1002/tl

of instructor, departmental chair, or college dean. Curriculum assessment of the integrated core, in a conscious formal process outside of departmental or disciplinary spaces, has become the means to take on many of these infrastructural questions, and to develop and deliver the content and share the academic goals of the ASCI core in between the cultures of the colleges who are collectively responsible for staffing this program.

For the most part, faculty assigned to teach in the ASCI core have been pleased to do so, because just as disciplinary administrative walls can create obstacles to cross-disciplinary quality control and assessment, they can also limit the teaching opportunities of more adventurous faculty, some of whom arrived with interdisciplinary training, others of whom are self-taught border crossers. For such self-selecting faculty, the ASCI core needs to be pedagogically and administratively hospitable, another crucial piece of content not accounted for in the variable-content structure (necessary for flexibility in staffing) of the BAS program as proposed and approved. When you are not part of the development or daily delivery of a curriculum but you parachute in to deliver a course, you may have trouble getting your bearings: you don't know what the students have studied to date, or how; you don't know the level of difficulty or challenge that you can expect students to meet; you can't walk down the hall and chat with the person who last taught this course or the courses that preceded it, given that even spatially the campus does not encourage the two cultures to meet; and so on. Curriculum assessment provides a culture in which both students and faculty between cultures can find a curricular home.

Stages and Means of Curriculum Assessment

When I became the chair of the BAS Program Committee, I was at sea, or, as one of the committee members said of herself at her first meeting, "I feel like I've walked in in the middle of the movie." I knew that the program was new, I knew that the students were really keen and a seemingly different breed from most incoming undergraduates, I knew that this was the program that would make good on Akademia's curtailed promise. I also knew (because students came to tell me) that teaching and course design were quite uneven in the ASCI core, yet my evidence was only anecdotal: I had no power to assign nor any jurisdiction to supervise ASCI faculty, or to see course evaluations of faculty teaching in the program; and I was dependent on the good will of the deans of all colleges across campus to provide faculty whose interests and expertise were appropriate to the integrated (but not widely known) purpose of the ASCI core.

Under these circumstances, and given that the BAS was created because of the Akademia students' needs, I decided to go to the students themselves to get a sense of what in any other program would simply be taken for granted (where people had seen the movie so many times, they knew the story from beginning to end, or thought they did). What did the students themselves expect when they chose the BAS program, and was the program meeting their expectations? I designed a questionnaire to poll the students' views and begin to accrue a critical mass of material from which to flesh out the structural skeleton of the BAS program, to formalize the feedback on the program, and from there to work more systematically on curriculum assessment and development. The results would (I hoped) facilitate informed faculty recruitment, informed decanal commitment, and pedagogical success for faculty and students alike.

The questionnaire (winter 2004) was electronic, open only to BAS students, and anonymous, and sought qualitative data (questions were designed to solicit written answers, and typical to this cohort of students, they had plenty to say). The questions were:

1. Why did you choose the BAS program (rather than a BA or a BSc program)?
2. What do you plan to do with (or after) your degree?
3. What values do you hope to develop or nurture as a student of arts and sciences?
4. What skill sets do you hope to develop or expect to have on completion of the BAS program?
5. How is this program different (or how should it be different) from a liberal arts degree? From a sciences degree? Should all courses (not just ASCI) be specifically designed for students in this program? Or would it dilute the value of the program for students to attend different courses from other arts students (for your BA minor) and other sciences students (for the BSc minor)?

Equipped with the findings of this poll, with student representation on the BAS Program Committee, and with the good academic will of the dean of the College of Arts to approve the hire of a new tenure-track historian of science (40 percent of whose teaching per year would be dedicated to the ASCI core and the remainder to the history department), I now had quite a bit of "content" with which to work. I also had access to two of the faculty members who had cotaught Akademia courses—indeed, the first ASCI offerings were renditions of these courses taught by these same faculty (a philosopher-bioethicist and a drama professor). I also had access to a faculty member appointed jointly between history and philosophy (whose expertise was science as a field), and another between philosophy and psychology (whose expertise was mind and cognition). With such good actual and potential material at hand, and with growing enrollments requiring longer-term planning for delivering more sections of ASCI courses than initially anticipated, I had a preliminary piece of what I needed to get the deans' collective attention. I prepared a framework document for a spring

2005 discussion with the deans titled "Endorsing a University-Wide Commitment to Resourcing the BAS Program." The document recommended action on several fronts, especially for the means to "translate" the proposed coherence and structural integrity of the program from the variable-content ASCI calendar copy into a quality schedule of studies whose content could be guaranteed—and guaranteed to be integrated ASCI. But many of my "asks" trespassed into the difficult terrain of questioning the quality of faculty expertise and instruction and the fiscal decision making of independent disciplinary or college-owned units. Again, curriculum assessment would be a means of passing through these cultural barriers.

My most pressing objective with this deans' document was to get their commitment to provide faculty for the delivery of what would be more than a dozen ASCI course sections (with more than half of these at the fourth-year seminar level) to accommodate the numbers of students in the program by 2006–07. Any further work on the curriculum required a critical mass of faculty to engage and feedback from students with access to a broader disciplinary range of faculty than had been available in the first two years of the program's operation. But I also needed more up-to-date feedback from students, which is where teaching support services came to the rescue, particularly in the form of the formal curriculum assessment package developed by Peter Wolf and others (as discussed in Chapter Two).

In winter 2006 Wolf and the BAS program counselor ran focus groups with first- and fourth-year students and surveyed the small pool of graduates to seek qualitative data on their views of the characteristics of the ideal BAS graduate, on the strengths and weaknesses of their program, and what they perceived as opportunities for and threats to fulfilling the program's potential. The student focus group process was followed by Wolf using the same questions to run another focus group, this one comprising BAS Program Committee members and as many past, current, and prospective instructors of ASCI courses as could attend a meeting. After the data were collected, the faculty–program committee perspective was compared to the data collected from the student focus groups. The results were remarkably similar for each question, considering that we had not had these kinds of meta-level discussions about the program in any sustained way before, and several of us had not developed or taught an ASCI course, but had served on the BAS Program Committee.

The good news was that we collectively believed in and were delivering a more coherent and integrated ASCI core than I had thought we were (and than might have been anticipated by the 2004 questionnaire, though it too was more good news than otherwise). The to-be-expected news was that we could do more with clearer and more broadly based decanal and faculty commitment to the program, and we must stabilize the quality of ASCI instruction and ASCI course content. The really good news was that I now had another significant batch of curriculum assessment results that showed this program was worth continued and further investment, and Wolf and I were able (in summer of

2006) to find a place at the Vice-President's Advisory Council (VPAC) table to report the findings and make the pitch for commitment—this time with data.

Concrete Infrastructural Results from Curriculum Assessment

The number of faculty assigned to teach ASCI courses has been growing steadily, and students have had access to a broader disciplinary representation in their ASCI faculty than in the early days of the program. The dean of arts has just hired another interdisciplinarian, 60 percent of whose teaching and service is dedicated to the BAS program, the rest to her home department; the dean of social and applied human sciences has received funding under a university-wide integrated plan to hire another such person in the next calendar year; the dean of biological sciences plans to make two similar hires in his college over the next few years; and with those models I hope to leverage similar appointments out of the remaining colleges across campus. The home unit gets a piece of a person that they hire and the BAS gets the rest; other designated and assigned BAS faculty get another colleague with whom they share the same keen and keenly different ASCI students. And all of them participate in ongoing curriculum assessment, insofar as assessment work to date becomes the foundation for informing each new person who is assigned to teach in the program. Already the historian of science (the first BAS-dedicated hire)—who has taught both the first semester foundational ASCI 1000 (Science and Society: Historical Perspectives) and the capstone ASCI 4000 and 4010 (honors research and thesis courses)—has made plans to meet with the pathologist assigned from the veterinary college, who has been teaching the foundational second semester ASCI 1010 (Science and Society: Contemporary Perspectives). Together they will be redeveloping the first-year ASCI experience based on their actual (and repeated) teaching experiences in the program and in the context of the questions asked and data collected in the curriculum assessment process.

Meanwhile, I dream of an extended repeat of a mini–course design institute that Wolf and I organized just before the fall 2006 semester. We gathered several of the ASCI faculty assigned to teach in the fall term in one room to share our individually developed course plans: we spelled out our explicit learning objectives, discovered the implicit ones, compared notes on the level of difficulty and type of skill development that we expected for our courses, and predicted how we thought our methods of evaluation addressed all these criteria. This mini–course design institute was not just a bonding opportunity for ASCI faculty in a "get-pumped" session to start the term (though more such opportunities are needed for everyone): it was also, once again, a form of curriculum assessment and a preparation for further assessment. The good news was that like the other stages of assessment, this stage produced remarkably similar results and a high degree of consensus around the room;

NEW DIRECTIONS FOR TEACHING AND LEARNING • DOI: 10.1002/tl

the to-be-expected news was that we all agreed that we need more of this kind of integrated individual course development, which will facilitate integrated curriculum development, and we need the ongoing input of student curriculum assessment, not just course assessment, to keep us honest.

Conclusion: The Benefits of Coming in during the Middle of the Movie

A program experiment like the bachelor of arts and sciences is significantly different from the more usual interdisciplinary program structure, which depends entirely on students fulfilling a schedule of studies from courses already on offer, already staffed, and already accounted for in administrative and fiscal terms. It is also significantly different from disciplinary programs, where the introduction of variable-content courses (especially at the upper levels of the curriculum, often introduced for flexibility of staffing under reduced budgets) rests at least on a shared sense of what students can be expected to know and do by that point in their program. But the complications of contemporary university life—particularly the compression of time into increased workloads, the depletion of capacity from decreased resources, the accompanying astonishment that enrollments continue to rise in almost all programs, the imperative to bring in research dollars from external sources, and the sheer growth of knowledge in all fields—mean that conversations about teaching and about curriculum are rare for any program. Meaningful course design as curricular design requires time for reflection, comparison, and research on teaching and learning that we just do not seem to have, again regardless of program or department or college home. But individual course development and delivery can be informed, and a different culture of curriculum development and delivery introduced, if you get a group of faculty and students engaged in a formal curriculum assessment. If it has been so successful for people in such an administratively attenuated program core, imagine how powerful it can be in a location where people are on the same page, as it were.

When I look at newer colleagues entering the profession and I look at colleagues who have been professors for many years in long-standing disciplinary and interdisciplinary programs, I wonder, though, if we haven't always been walking in in the middle of a movie or if we've ever been watching the same movie at all, regardless of when we came in. Working on the ASCI core of the BAS program has been highly useful for defamiliarizing the infrastructural issues embedded in all curricular development and delivery. Curriculum assessment not only brings to light what is left implicit in a curriculum but also exposes an institutional unconsciousness of the daily complexities of curriculum development and delivery. It has brought home how "acculturated" we are, how much we continue to take for granted, how much remains implicit in more typical programs, and how very atomistic course development and delivery too often are—an individual's expertise or research interest is poured into a course that he "owns," rather

NEW DIRECTIONS FOR TEACHING AND LEARNING • DOI: 10.1002/tl

than being composed as a consciously planned solo (or duet, trio, or quartet, even), in a consciously orchestrated production.

At this stage of the program's operation, ASCI course development and delivery continue to be more atomistic than collective, which means that curricular assessment and development for such an administratively attenuated core will clearly be an ongoing and required venture, not just the more typical periodic checkup on what we think of as more organic developments in the shared climate of a department, discipline, or college. But we are evolving: the BAS Program Committee now has more members who have taught ASCI courses than in the past, and they are there not to represent college or disciplinary turf but to represent and to work on the unique ASCI aspects of the program. I know that when I go hunting for faculty for ASCI course delivery, I will actually find them, and their deans and chairs will not expect a buy-out and will not treat ASCI teaching as something lesser than what happens in their home unit. I also know, as a result of reporting on the curriculum assessment process to the provost's advisory council, that I can get student feedback on the program through an approved, separately reported section added to the standardized course evaluation form for ASCI courses: individual ASCI course and ASCI instructor feedback remains confidential to faculty and to their performance review committees (per faculty policy), whereas program-specific feedback is now collected course by course for use in ongoing curriculum assessment and development. This and other "bonus features" of the BAS movie are easily adaptable to other films coming to a department or program near you.

DONNA PALMATEER PENNEE is professor in the School of English and Theatre Studies and associate dean of Arts and Social Sciences at the University of Guelph.

NEW DIRECTIONS FOR TEACHING AND LEARNING • DOI: 10.1002/tl

7

This chapter introduces a comprehensive model of curricular evolution and assessment at the faculty level as developed and implemented in a core program at Renaissance College, University of New Brunswick.

The University of New Brunswick's Renaissance College: Curricular Evolution and Assessment at the Faculty Level

Pierre Zundel, Thomas Mengel

Stimulating the evolution of teaching and learning was the main motivation for the University of New Brunswick (UNB) to launch the process of creating a new faculty called Renaissance College (RC) in 1998. UNB is a doctoral and research university of 11,000 students operating in the eastern Canadian province of New Brunswick. RC has proven highly effective. In 2006, the college received the Society for Teaching and Learning in Higher Education's national Alan K. Blizzard Award for collaborative teaching. As further evidence of success, one of RC's core programs—the Bachelor of Philosophy in Interdisciplinary Leadership Studies (BPhil) program—has consistently placed over 70 percent of its graduates in a wide range of top graduate and professional programs in North America, including some Ivy League universities in the United States.

The purpose of this chapter is to draw some general lessons on curricular evolution processes and practices at the faculty level emerging from the creation of RC and the implementation of its BPhil program. We proceed by induction, working from the specific case of Renaissance College to a general model of curricular evolution and its associated processes. In the process, we describe the direction setting, assessment, and capacity building processes used in curricular evolution, illustrating them with two specific examples from the BPhil program: the use of learning portfolios and the

teaching of structured problem solving. Finally, we present general observations about curricular evolution for faculties or institutions. We will argue from our experience that effective curricular evolution requires commitment to the following key ideas:

- Explicit student learning outcomes, organizational values, and beliefs are essential for curricular design and assessment.
- Curricular design and development is not only a top-down, hierarchical process, but also a bottom-up, organic and cultural one that needs to be supported in different ways by all members of the community.
- At the faculty level, curriculum evolution can explicitly consider features that are "fixed" at the program or course level.
- A focus on curricular assessment at all levels and involving all participants (for example, faculty, students, and community members) is critical to success.
- Faculty research about their teaching—the scholarship of teaching and learning (SoTL)—is an essential component in informing, guiding, and enabling the process of curricular evolution.
- Appropriate recruitment, selection, mentoring, and support of faculty members are essential to effective implementation of the approach we describe.

Program Components

In this section we outline RC's program components, which comprise learning outcomes, outcomes courses, integrated forum courses, leadership stream, internship placements, disciplinary minor, college life activities, and learning portfolios.

Learning Outcomes. In the Renaissance College Learning Outcomes Guide (Renaissance College, 2005), each outcome is described in both conceptual and operational terms, the latter being expressly created to provide guidance to faculty in developing what Wolf, Hill, and Evers (2006) call "course objectives." It is our assumption that when students have mastered these outcomes in the content of the courses and in their own experiences, they will have the abilities, knowledge, and attitudes needed for effective leadership. The development of leadership potential through a liberal education is the main purpose of the college (Renaissance College, 2006). In this way, the learning outcomes are the operational description of the educational goal of the institution or what Wolf, Hill, and Evers (2006) refer to as "programme objectives" (p. 7).

The Renaissance College learning outcomes (RCLOs) are

Effective citizenship: the ability to assess community needs on various levels and take effective and appropriate action informed by one's own values and those of the community

Knowing oneself and others: The ability to describe one's own worldview and that of others and to link this understanding to taking action in the private and public spheres

Multiliteracy: the ability to effectively provide and interpret information in a variety of forms and formats (for example, the written and spoken word, nonverbal communication, virtual communication, numeracy, and aesthetic responsiveness)

Personal well-being: the ability to analyze one's status using a conceptual framework for physical, emotional, spiritual, and intellectual well-being and to work effectively alone and in groups to enhance well-being

Problem solving: the ability to solve problems in a structured way that is appropriate to the context, both individually and in groups

Social interaction: the ability to work effectively with others in task-oriented situations as well as deal with interpersonal problems and to use social interaction as a means of increasing understanding of complex situations

Rather than using a traditional smorgasbord of individual courses, the program offers a wide range of linked program components to help students grow in the learning outcomes. These components reflect the combination of the learning outcomes with our educational philosophy and values as described in the RC vision document (Renaissance College, 2006). The values and beliefs held in the college create a collaborative, problem-based, experiential, reflective, and active pedagogy. The program components are described next.

Outcomes Courses. Early in the program, students take several courses introducing particular learning outcomes. For example, in the course Mathematical and Economic Approaches to Problem Solving students are introduced to the structured problem-solving model and practice solving problems of growing complexity and difficulty. They receive feedback based on criteria describing in detail the various components of the problem-solving model. Student performance data gathered during the course allow us to track growth in student problem-solving ability (Kuruganti and Zundel, 2004). Various courses introduce the other RCLOs in a similar approach.

Integrated Forum Courses. Students also take one forum course in each semester integrating the learning from various outcome-focused courses by working on challenging interdisciplinary and community problems. For example, students might be asked to prepare briefs to a simulated royal commission on aboriginal access to natural resources or to present recommendations on the implementation of a provincial health initiative to a real panel of experts in the field. In this context of group projects and presentations, all outcomes are further developed.

Leadership Stream. Students also take five leadership courses introducing them to leadership theory and practice. The learning and assessment in these courses focuses on the RCLOs that are most appropriate for each course (for example, effective citizenship is emphasized in the course Leadership and

Public Policy). Furthermore, students take the lead in particular projects and engage in reflective practices and self-development.

Internship Placements. During the summer students participate in internships in Canada and overseas. The Canadian internship allows students to work with a leader-mentor in a public or private organization and see leadership in action, analyze organizational culture, and develop in several of the learning outcomes for which they set goals in advance. International internships of twelve weeks' duration take place overseas, usually in developing countries. Students are placed with a wide variety of organizations in situations providing a high degree of interaction with citizens of the host country. This experience provides excellent opportunities for students to grow in all RCLOs, but particularly in "knowing oneself and others" and in observing firsthand the relationship between culture and leadership practices.

Disciplinary Minor. Students are required to take a minor to provide them some depth in a specific discipline. The diversity of minors also contributes to the intellectual richness of discussions and group work in RC courses.

College Life Activities. The college hosts a wide range of cocurricular activities creating opportunities for students to learn about the outcomes in nontraditional contexts and building a safe and challenging community of learning. Some examples of activities include managing a small organic garden adjacent to the college to produce food for the weekly communal meal and for the local soup kitchen; coffeehouses raising funds for women's shelters; invited speakers series; and publishing *The Troubadour,* a student newspaper. In addition, students are heavily involved in college governance bodies such as the faculty council, the undergraduate research lab, and the research ethics board. Students are strongly encouraged to use their participation and learning in these and other cocurricular activities as evidence of growing competency in the learning outcomes.

Learning Portfolio. Throughout their program, students are expected to develop a learning portfolio that documents their growth and competency in the six RCLOs. One portfolio course in each year of the program guides the students through this process and helps them become self-aware learners and develop self-assessment skills. It also serves to integrate the learning they do in a wide range of academic and cocurricular contexts. The portfolio process culminates in the public presentation of one learning outcome and the evaluation of the whole portfolio by multiple faculty members and one external community assessor at the end of their program. The use of external assessors motivates students to do their best and also helps the college calibrate its expectations and assess the success of its program.

Curricular Evolution Processes

The college has used a number of curriculum development processes since the start of the program. Figure 7.1 identifies the components, connec-

NEW DIRECTIONS FOR TEACHING AND LEARNING • DOI: 10.1002/tl

tions, and processes involved in institutional and curricular evolution. The central column represents the evolutionary processes from the institutional (top row) to the course level (bottom row), showing how each stage's output informs the next level. The right-hand column presents the various types of monitoring and assessment carried out to inform curricular and institutional change. The left-hand column shows the relationships between scholarship, faculty development, and curricular change. Between the components in each row are cyclic processes for the development of strategic direction, programs, outcomes, and courses (shown as *a* to *d* in Figure 7.1) utilizing feedback from students, faculty, and external sources. The activity level and speed of cycling is greatest at the level of course development and slowest in visioning. Episodic changes in the vision lead to substantial ripple effects in program and course evolution. The following sections illustrate how these

Figure 7.1. Context for Curriculum Evolution

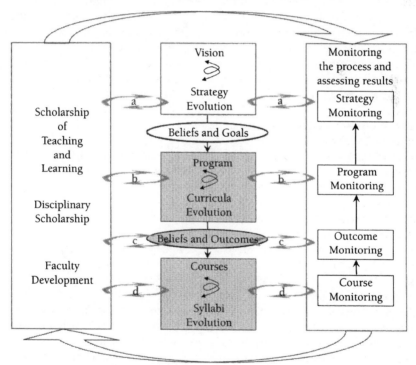

Legend: ▭ Kirkpatrick's (1998) "Four Levels   a: Strategy Development Cycle
of Evalution" and Wolf's (2005)   b: Program Development Cycle
"Curriculum Development Process"   c: Outcome Development Cycle
focus on the areas shaded in this   d: Course Development Cycle
diagram.

various processes and influences play out for our two examples, the learning portfolio and the teaching of problem solving.

Visioning and Strategic Planning Processes. The college is one of eleven faculties at UNB's Fredericton campus. The College Council is the "legislative" body responsible for approving curriculum change proposals and setting local policy (for example, defining course learning outcomes). The UNB Fredericton Senate must approve substantial changes to course descriptions and program requirements. Faculty deans are given substantial autonomy to manage their units within constraints imposed by collective agreements and Senate and Board of Governors policies on academic and resources issues. Faculties submit academic plans (including reports on key indicators and initiatives) as part of the annual planning and budgeting process.

The college has gone through three visioning exercises since its creation in 1998. The first of these was the initiation of the college to pursue the development of an undergraduate interdisciplinary leadership program with the help of donor funding (Roderick and others, 2006). A group of approximately fifty faculty members from the two main UNB campuses developed the vision and curriculum for this new program, which was approved by the UNB Senate early in 2000. This initial design included a vision statement and a first document outlining the learning outcomes for the BPhil program (Zundel and others, 2000). Finally, it created a diverse set of learning activities that would help its students achieve the learning outcomes. One critical structure that emerged from this process was the learning portfolio described earlier (though initially without associated courses). All courses were then designed and delivered by a diverse group of faculty members seconded to the college.

After its launch, the college underwent a second and third direction-setting episode. In the second, a quality assurance self-study and subsequent external review in 2003–04 affirmed the original design but also broadened its educational offerings with two additional programs and recommended hiring a core group of college faculty members (Renaissance College, 2004; Engelmann, Bisson, and Harker, 2004).

The third and most recent vision-strategy-development process followed the hiring of core faculty members (including Thomas Mengel) and a new dean (Pierre Zundel). This broadly based strategic planning process was initiated in 2005, resulting in a substantially revised vision document for the college as well as some strategic goals for the curriculum (Mengel, 2007). In essence, RC's vision is based on the joint values of an active, holistic, and interdisciplinary learning culture; leadership; community; mindful openness; excellence; and congruence. The following were identified as the main reasons for the existence of Renaissance College:

- Our primary purpose is to nurture and develop leadership potential and engaged citizenship through the liberal education of our students.

- We are a learning community focused on experimenting with and modeling highly effective, innovative teaching and learning practices, citizenship, and leadership.
- We improve postsecondary education by engaging in the scholarship of teaching and learning (Renaissance College, 2006).

The top two boxes in the middle column of Figure 7.1 represent the majority of the activities included in all three visioning exercises. Planning at this level also allows some of the elements contained in "university context" referred to by Wolf, Hill, and Evers (2006) to be explicitly integrated with design of formal curriculum (p.7). For example, College Life activities are routinely used by students in their portfolios as evidence for competency in certain learning outcomes. Some of the major strategic directions that link to the processes outlined in Figure 7.1 include a focus on undergraduate education; on SoTL as the major RC contribution to research; on a need to review the structure and functioning of each of the components of the programs we offer; and on monitoring both progress toward the strategic goals and the wellness of RC community members.

Assessment and Redesign Processes. A culture of continuous assessment has evolved at RC since its inception. The right-hand column in Figure 7.1 describes the various levels of assessment. To gather information about the student perspective on courses, we use formal university-designed student opinion surveys; custom-designed, detailed feedback instruments on individual course components; and midcourse temperature checks. These are combined with faculty assessment of student work in those courses and of their progress toward the RCLOs (Kuruganti and Zundel, 2004). Each semester faculty synthesize this information and, together with the dean, they review results and make plans for changes to their courses as part of the course development cycle (see Figure 7.1, cycle d). During the latter process, data gathered inform program-level changes (for example, trends in student performance at problem solving).

Each cohort of students holds debriefing sessions at the end of each year to provide input to formal curricular change and to college life activities at the program level. These sessions are supplemented in real time throughout the year by monthly reports from representatives of each cohort to the College Council. The information gathered from these various sources is used in faculty program development workshops (described later in this section) and for real-time changes in curriculum delivery. In the original BPhil program design, the learning portfolio was a requirement for graduation, but no formal course credit was given for it, and no course time slot existed to provide guidance about its development. Feedback received from the cohorts of students graduating in 2003 and 2004 led to the creation of formal courses for portfolio development, with subsequent improvements in portfolio quality and reductions in student stress levels.

As part of outcome monitoring and assessment, student performance in third-year portfolio presentations and written documents is evaluated by faculty and external assessors, and judgments are rendered on the degree to which students as a group are demonstrating growth and competency in the RCLO. For example, in 2006 faculty and external assessments indicated that students were not providing compelling evidence of their ability to carry out the implementation and evaluation phases of the problem-solving model. This discovery has led to changes in the curriculum—for example, restructuring the third-year Community Problem Solving course to allow students to participate in implementation and monitoring of projects on which they work in the course.

Periodic reviews of major program components are also undertaken. A review of the leadership stream of courses was begun in 2005–06 (Mengel, 2006b) and will be finalized in 2007. Learning portfolios will again be reviewed in 2008, once the impact modifications made in 2005–06 can be assessed. Although these reviews have historically been motivated by needs identified as a result of student feedback, performance issues, or instructor concerns, the strategic planning process described earlier has increasing influence on the curricular review process (for example, sequencing program review activities).

In addition to these formal curricular assessment processes, SoTL projects by faculty provide additional information about the program (Kuruganti and Zundel, 2004; Valk and Alberts, 2005; Roderick and others, 2006). In one project, portfolio course instructors identified substantial issues related to student performance in the outcomes (Reeves, Roderick, and Zundel, 2005). These observations led to course and student feedback modifications, with resultant increases in the quality of portfolios submitted in 2006. This change is represented in Figure 7.1 in the left-hand version of the course development cycle d.

One of the main vehicles to create new designs and modify the curriculum has been the use of thrice-yearly program development workshops (in May, August, and December). At these two- to three-day sessions, issues at the faculty level are discussed, assessment information is reviewed, and solutions are created. This process focuses on cycles b and c in Figure 7.1. It includes workload leveling for students, developing common theme topics, considering the recommendations of major reviews, and developing assessment policies. Facilitation by faculty members, common meals, and productive collaborative work during these workshops all contribute to community building within RC.

Capacity-Building Processes. Another key component in curriculum evolution has been to continually grow the capacity of our faculty and staff (see Figure 7.1, left-hand column). In 2006–07, this growth included invited workshops and presentations by a senior scholar from the Carnegie Academy for the Scholarship of Teaching and Learning, faculty from the Harvard

Business School, and Alverno College. In addition, the college sponsored a joint trip to Alverno College to learn more about outcome-based teaching and assessment. This experience resulted in the creation of a matrix of courses and learning outcomes to identify gaps and excessive coverage of the outcomes in the program. During the subsequent faculty workshop, this matrix was used to determine which outcomes would need to be taught and assessed in each course and how to make the series of courses for each outcome developmental. Follow-up on the trip continues at the time of writing and feeds into closing the loop on this process through assessment and monitoring of courses and outcomes (see Figure 7.1, cycles c and d). This follow-up will determine the success of the designs created and links faculty development to curriculum evolution. In addition, traditional disciplinary scholarship of faculty members informs both the growing subject matter expertise of faculty and the review processes of individual courses and whole program streams (such as the leadership stream review mentioned earlier).

Key Ideas

A number of key ideas about curriculum evolution emerge. First, the importance of intentionality involves being clear about our faculty and program objectives and who our students are, designing curriculum around these two factors, and assessing our success in reaching those objectives. Consistent student learning outcomes at the faculty, program, course, and course activity level provide the foundation for all design, assessment, and redesign.

Second, in our experience, the process of design and assessment does not always proceed top-down from the program-level perspective to the course level. Often faculty members' scholarship and experience of teaching inform and influence program- and faculty-level objectives. For example, the recent review of the leadership stream of courses or the changes to the portfolio process were driven by concerns emerging at the level of individual courses or in faculty members' SoTL work, rather than being mandated by a program-level curricular review model. The evolution of the curriculum and its associated pedagogies, then, is as much cultural and organic as it is managerial and structured. While the two approaches strengthen each other, they also require a tolerance for ambiguity and procedural untidiness, both of which can be challenging. It implies a need to feel comfortable with a style of leadership that encourages and accommodates self-organization and complex, systemic change initiatives (Wheatley, 1999) and applies emotional and spiritual intelligence (Goleman, Boyatzis, and McKee, 2004; Zohar and Marshall, 2001; Mengel, 2005, 2006a). The trust among colleagues created by frequent collaborative teaching, planning, scholarly activity, and participation in the learning community makes it easier to find this tolerance.

Third, assessment at every level and by all participants (faculty and staff, students, administrators, and external assessors) in the curriculum is also a key component of curriculum evolution. It is particularly powerful when it is carried out in the context of clear learning outcomes and institutional goals, values, and philosophies. As described earlier and illustrated in Figure 7.1, we exert considerable effort at formal and informal assessment of curriculum, student performance relative to the learning outcomes, and student perceptions of the program. This assessment informs and guides curriculum evolution and visioning.

Fourth, setting up a curriculum assessment process at the faculty and program level to help gather qualitative as well as quantitative data and to understand and improve the effectiveness of the curriculum (Wolf, Hill, and Evers, 2006) is a valuable first step. Placing it in a curriculum development process based on the program objectives and competencies (Wolf, Hill, and Evers, 2006) and including a detailed model of evaluation (Kirkpatrick, 1998) make this process even more meaningful. However, our experiences have informed the development of an even more comprehensive model and approach (see Figure 7.1). Program development and assessment need to be organically and dynamically integrated into the context of vision and strategy development, the monitoring of processes and assessment of results at various levels, and the engagement of faculty in the scholarship of teaching and learning as well as in other faculty development initiatives. In particular, the development cycles at the strategy, program, outcome, and course level (Figure 7.1, cycles *a* through *d*) need to link the hierarchical evolution processes at the strategy, program, and course level (center column of Figure 7.1) to the dynamic assessment, scholarship, and faculty development systems. Curriculum development and assessment thus grow from a one-time curricular design activity and closed system into a continuously looping process that is part of a larger, organically developing system of organizational development and assessment.

Fifth, the scholarship of teaching and learning serves the local need for scholarly reflection on the college's curriculum and sets it in a broader context of scholarly work on postsecondary education in general. It brings best practices into the curriculum design and redesign process. It also submits values, philosophies, assumptions, and interpretations to critical review by peers, ensuring that curricular design is based on the best possible thinking. SoTL also serves a broader purpose of helping others involved in curriculum evolution benefit from the experience gained at the college.

Finally, the recruitment, selection, mentoring, and support of faculty are critically important. Our academic staff comprises a small number of tenured full- and part-time (jointly appointed) faculty, as well as seconded and stipendiary instructors. Our faculty recruitment and selection process explicitly gathers information on faculty interests in interdisciplinary learning, team teaching, scholarship of teaching and learning, and other key activities in which they would be involved in the college. Once hired, our faculty are mentored and supported through a range of processes such as

NEW DIRECTIONS FOR TEACHING AND LEARNING • DOI: 10.1002/tl

joint professional development, thrice yearly curriculum workshops, joint research projects, and teaching in teams with experienced faculty. Furthermore, all our faculty, regardless of their type of appointment, participate in the governance and development processes that are part of the collaborative scholarly work of the college. Faculty are involved in the generation and maintenance of the culture that supports curricular innovation.

Sustaining the Process

Supporting the culture of assessment and curriculum evolution requires substantial investment by positional leaders. This investment comes in a variety of forms. One of the most important is to hire faculty with a passion for teaching and an interest in working as collaborators in a learning community, rather than as rugged individualists. Leaders also help the community articulate its values and vision and then systematically use these to guide curricular choices. The disciplined and consistent modeling of these values and vision is critical. Equally necessary is the investment of time and scarce resources to create and participate in the occasions for team building, collaborative reflection on the curriculum, pedagogy, and student learning and, in some cases, to pay sessional instructors to participate in them (for example, cohort debriefings, curriculum development workshops, and faculty development activities). Finally, positional leaders need to run interference for their faculty as they experiment with new approaches, some of which will either fail or meet with initial resistance.

The process of curricular evolution is also supported by the work of faculty. Experienced faculty and staff work with newer members to help them integrate key components of the assessment approach (for example, outcome-based assessment) and become active scholars of teaching and learning by coauthoring papers on themes of common interest. Faculty also take personal risks (in the tenure and promotion process, for example) in discussing their pedagogical challenges and in attempting new approaches to teaching. These risks are supported by positional leaders through the relationships of trust built among colleagues and through the collective experience that helps faculty shape their innovations and manage risks. The process of course planning and delivery is informed by a rich flow of information from a variety of sources. Faculty know more specifically how their course contributes to the learning outcomes at the heart of the curriculum—knowledge that helps with, and also adds a level of complexity to, course design. The frequent discussions and collaboration about teaching also provide a wide range of models and ideas about teaching methods, tools, and approaches. This breadth of choice creates an environment that is simultaneously challenging and supportive.

Students also support the process in a number of ways. They contribute time and effort as they participate in the variety of direction setting, assessment, and reflection activities in courses, as cohorts and as members of the College Council and its working groups (for example, the Strategic Assessment Team). As their input is integrated into the curriculum and practices of the college, they gain confidence in the value of their time investment. In addition, students are frequently asked to participate as subjects in research about teaching and as coresearchers (for example, in our Undergraduate Research Lab on Leadership Education). This sort of engagement requires a change in student perception of their role from client or recipient of education to partner in its creation. This change in attitude is sometimes challenging.

Challenges

In order to be substantial rather than trivial, outcomes-based learning needs to focus on rich, complex learning outcomes that bring together skills and attitudes with disciplinary content (Alverno College faculty, 1992). This focus requires keeping an appropriate balance between depth or richness and feasibility of assessment. Many faculty and students have been trained and educated in an academic culture whose primary educational concern is the coverage of disciplinary content. Hence a focus on learning and teaching based on learning outcomes requires a fundamental change of thinking and practice. This change takes time and must initially be maintained by substantial mentoring, provision of models, and professional development.

The collaboration and development work associated with the culture of assessment and outcomes-based learning consumes substantial time; thus faculty workload becomes an issue. It is helpful that UNB explicitly recognizes SoTL as research in its collective agreement. In addition, the college has provided an increasing number of undergraduate and graduate teaching assistants to support the work of faculty in this environment. However, we recognize that providing excellence in teaching and learning is both a worthwhile endeavor and hard work. The challenge is maintaining a sustainable balance within and outside of the college.

Conclusion

We intentionally created and now maintain a system of organic and structured curriculum development and assessment processes and cycles. Learning outcomes are integral components of this comprehensive system. Our joint engagement in the scholarship of teaching and learning helps redefine our understanding and practice of a vibrant and sustainable community of learning and teaching. Our culture of collaboration supports these approaches.

External reviews of the program in 2004 indicated that "every one of the approximately twenty-five students and alumnae who were interviewed demonstrated an impressive ability to articulate what and how they learned, and to argue for the rigour and validity of their educational experience." While this model comes with a time cost that remains a challenge, it has been effective for RC and its environment, as indicated by the Alan Blizzard Award for collaborative teaching as well as by the postgraduation success of its alumni.

References

Alverno College faculty. *Liberal Learning at Alverno College.* Milwaukee, Wis.: Alverno College Productions, 1992.

Engelmann, D., Bisson, B., and Harker, J. "Renaissance College University of New Brunswick External Review Report." Unpublished document, Renaissance College, 2004.

Goleman, D., Boyatzis, R., and McKee, A. *Primal Leadership: Learning to Lead with Emotional Intelligence.* Boston: Harvard Business School Press, 2004.

Kirkpatrick, D. *Evaluating Training Programs: The Four Levels.* San Francisco: Berrett-Koehler, 1998.

Kuruganti, U., and Zundel, P. E. "Teaching Quantitative Skills Using Repeated Problem Solving Exercises Combined with Explicit Learning Outcomes." In S. Le-May Sheffield, C. O'Neil, K. L. Taylor, and D. Nevo (eds.), *Proceedings of the Atlantic Teaching Showcase,* Dalhousie University, Halifax, Nova Scotia, Oct. 2004.

Mengel, T. "Wisdom and Knowledge: Leadership in Balance." *Positive Living E-Zine,* June 7, 2005.

Mengel, T. "From Making a Living to Making a Life:—Leadership Development Revisited." *i-Manager's Journal of Management,* 2006a, *1*(2), 35–41.

Mengel, T. "Leading into the Future?—A Review of Renaissance College's Leadership Curriculum." In J. Hoyle, P. Nelson, and N. L. Pitts (eds.), *Atlantic Universities Teaching Showcase 2005.* Truro, N.S.: Nova Scotia Agricultural College, 2006b.

Mengel, T. "Values and Voices at Renaissance College: The Story of the Vision Quest and Learning Journey at UNB's Leadership School." *Atlantic Universities Teaching Showcase 2006.* St. Johns, NL: Memorial University of Newfoundland, 2007.

Reeves, V., Roderick, C., and Zundel, P. E. "Assessing Student Growth and Competency: The Renaissance College Approach." Paper presented at 2005 Annual Meeting of the Society for Teaching and Learning in Higher Education, University of Prince Edward Island, Charlottetown, June 2005.

Renaissance College. "Renaissance College UNB Quality Assurance Program Self-Study Review." Unpublished document, Renaissance College, 2004.

Renaissance College. "Learning Outcomes Guide." Fredericton, N.B.: Renaissance College, 2005. Retrieved Jan. 31, 2007, from www.unb.ca/renaissance/news/documents/OutcomesDocumentDec05.pdf.

Renaissance College. "Vision and Strategy of Renaissance College." Unpublished document, Renaissance College, 2006.

Roderick, C., and others. "Renaissance College: Outcomes at the Whole Program Level." (Alan K. Blizzard Award paper.) Society for Teaching and Learning in Higher Education and McGraw Hill, 2006. Retrieved Feb. 23, 2007, from www.mcmaster.ca/stlhe/awards/2006%20Blizzard%20UNB.pdf.

Valk, J., and Alberts, N. "Know Thyself: Reflecting on and Deepening Personal Worldviews as Part of Student Learning." Paper presented at 2005 Annual Meeting of the Society for Teaching and Learning in Higher Education, University of Prince Edward Island, Charlottetown, June 2005.

Wheatley, M. J. *Leadership and the New Science: Discovering Order in a Chaotic World.* San Francisco: Berrett-Koehler, 1999.

Wolf, P., Hill, A., and Evers, H. *Handbook for Curriculum Assessment.* Guelph, Ont.: University of Guelph, 2006.

Zohar, D., and Marshall, I. *SQ. Spiritual Intelligence: The Ultimate Intelligence.* London: Bloomsbury, 2001.

Zundel, P. E., and others. "Renaissance College Learning and Leadership Outcomes Guide." Fredericton, N.B.: Renaissance College, University of New Brunswick, 2000.

PIERRE ZUNDEL *is dean and professor at Renaissance College and has been involved in the college since its inception.*

THOMAS MENGEL *is associate professor of Leadership Studies at Renaissance College.*

NEW DIRECTIONS FOR TEACHING AND LEARNING • DOI: 10.1002/tl

8

This chapter describes and critiques the curriculum development process for the original six programs at the University of Guelph-Humber, a new institution developed by the University of Guelph and the Humber Institute of Technology and Advanced Learning.

Integrating Knowledge, Skills, and Values into the Curriculum Development Process at the University of Guelph-Humber

Frederick Evers, Janet Wolstenholme

The focus of this paper is the curriculum development process that led to the intentional integration of knowledge, skills, and values in every course at a newly created institution, the University of Guelph-Humber (G-H). Among the many unique features of G-H, the integration of theory and practice in each course is one of the most important. The G-H curriculum is not made up of two years of college and two years of university; rather, it is four years of integrated university and college material. Another unique feature is that students receive a degree from Guelph and a diploma from Humber in four years.

University of Guelph-Humber Programs

In May 2001, the senate of the University of Guelph and the board of governors of Humber College approved the University of Guelph-Humber's first three programs, in business, computing co-op, and media studies. Three additional programs—early childhood studies, family and community social services, and justice studies—were approved in 2002.

The joint diploma-degree programs match complementary strengths at Humber and Guelph. The programs are specifically designed to compress the time for students to graduate with diplomas and degrees so that the programs can be completed in four years. The joint venture offers students a

New Directions for Teaching and Learning, no. 112, Winter 2007 © Wiley Periodicals, Inc.
Published online in Wiley InterScience (www.interscience.wiley.com) • DOI: 10.1002/tl.300

83

first-rate, accessible education close to their homes. The programs seamlessly integrate the diploma and degree experience. Students save time and money through tuition and living costs, and employers can hire uniquely skilled graduates sooner.

Faculty at G-H are affiliated with departments from their home institutions at either Guelph or Humber.

Curriculum Development Process

Curriculum development for the original six programs at G-H started in early 2001 and was completed in 2005. A key principle was that we would not use courses "off the shelf"—all the courses would be created to meet the unique needs of G-H.

In order to bring the new curriculum to fruition, a curriculum development committee was struck, composed of members from both parent institutions. The committee was cochaired by a representative from both the college and the university. Frederick Evers represented Guelph on the committee, and Janet Wolstenholme acted as the curriculum coordinator and representative for the committee through the curriculum adoption process.

The curriculum development process started with the program heads. They lined up expert course developers to prepare the proposals. The course proposals contained a course template and detailed proposal, which in turn included information on learning objectives, the course description, course topics, methods of instruction, online activities, a description of the evaluation methods, and a list of resources needed for the course. Completed course proposals were brought to the curriculum development committee (CDC) for review before the institutional approval processes. The CDC consisted of the cochairs, program heads, and representatives from the Library and Learning Commons, Office of Open Learning, and General Education. This committee examined each proposal carefully, ensuring that it was complete and that the learning objectives matched the content and evaluation tools. The CDC could, and did, send proposals back to the course developer for additional detailed information or for reworking.

Once the CDC was satisfied with the course proposals, they were sent to the G-H joint program committee for review. This committee ensured that program and course development was progressing appropriately and served as a check on the course proposals. Once reviewed by the joint program committee, course proposals were submitted to the official approval processes at the two institutions.

Now that the programs are under way, maintenance of courses and programs in general is treated in the same way as regular changes, adds, and deletions from any department within the university system (through meetings of program committees, which forward updates to the administration for approval and adoption).

New Directions for Teaching and Learning • DOI: 10.1002/tl

At times the process of integrating the cultures of a college and a university was quite challenging. Each of the partnering institutions needed to satisfy well-established policies regarding curriculum and the use of faculty time. We encountered logistical issues such as the number of "contact" hours needed to teach some courses. Because colleges in Ontario are bound by strict union agreements and typically do not have access to the graduate teaching assistants available at universities, finding the most effective way to deliver some course content proved challenging. However, through the ingenuity of the CDC members, most issues were worked through and creative solutions were posed.

Learning Objectives. Consistent with the goal of integrating theory with practice in each course, learning objectives were declared for each course in terms of knowledge, skills, and values. While knowledge was primarily left to the disciplinary experts, twenty general skills and eight values were identified. They were developed from the *Generic/Employability Skills* employed by Humber College (Humber Institute of Technology and Advanced Learning, 2006), the University of Guelph's (2006) *Learning Objectives,* and the *Bases of Competence* skills model (Evers, Rush, and Berdrow, 1998). These skills are listed in Exhibit 8.1, and the values are given in Exhibit 8.2. (Definitions of the skills

Exhibit 8.1. Skills Learning Objectives

Personal Skills
  1. Personal organization and time management
  2. Responsibility
  3. Adaptability and learning
  4. Problem solving
  5. Resource management

Communication Skills
  6. Reading
  7. Writing
  8. Speaking
  9. Listening
  10. Communicating through evolving media

Mathematical and Computing Skills
  11. Mathematics
  12. Computer applications

Teamwork and Leadership Skills
  13. Teamwork and interpersonal
  14. Leadership and assertiveness
  15. Conflict management
  16. Decision making

Thinking Skills
  17. Research
  18. Critical thinking
  19. Responsible risk taking
  20. Creative thinking and visioning

Exhibit 8.2. Values Learning Objectives

Citizenship
1. Sense of historical development
2. Global understanding

Moral and Aesthetic Maturity
3. Moral maturity
4. Aesthetic maturity

Lifelong Learning
5. Understanding of forms of inquiry
6. Depth and breadth of understanding
7. Independence of thought
8. Love of learning

and values are available at www.tss.uoguelph.ca/resources/idres/GH%20 definitions%20of%20skills%20&%20values.pdf.)

In addition to the twenty general skills, students learn skills specific to their field of study; for example, how to write newspaper articles versus magazine pieces in the media program or how to construct a wireless network in the distributed computing co-op program.

Course developers were asked to consider which of the twenty skills and eight values they felt were most relevant to each course and how skill and value development could be achieved. Although no single course can cover all skills and all values, it was expected that across all of a program's core courses, all twenty skills and eight values would be addressed. This coverage was checked by preparing a matrix of skills and values learning objectives and crossing them with the programs' courses (see Exhibit 8.3 for an example). In this way gaps in coverage are easily noted. For example, it is evident in Exhibit 8.3 that conflict management and responsible risk taking are not covered in any first-year courses. Program leaders can then decide whether this is a problem and, if so, whether these skills are better assigned to upper-level courses.

The CDC paid particular attention to the language of the knowledge, skills, and values learning objectives to ensure they were measurable or demonstrable. Building in these criteria makes success in the individual course quantifiable and assessment possible.

In support of the achievement of these outcomes, all programs were expected to integrate some form of skills portfolio with demonstrated discipline appropriate expertise. Most have students compile a large portion of the reflective content during their field placement courses or senior capstone courses.

All the programs at G-H also have an experiential component. This practice is congruent with the requirements necessary for the diploma and takes the form of approximately 240 hours of workplace experience (through applied projects, field placements, and community service requirements), except in the case of the computing co-op program, which requires

Exhibit 8.3. Skills Matrix for First Year of Early Childhood Studies

Semester 1: Fall Courses

Skills	AHSS 1110 Intro Psych: Dynamics	AHSS 1130 Principles of Sociology	AHSS 1120 Intro Psych: Principles	ECS 1000 Creating Nurturing and Safe Environments for Young Children
1. Personal Organization and Time Management	✓	✓		✓
2. Responsibility	✓	✓	✓	
3. Adaptability	✓			
4. Problem Solving	✓			
5. Resource Management	✓	✓✓✓	✓	✓
6. Reading	✓	✓	✓✓	✓
7. Writing	✓✓			
8. Speaking	✓✓			
9. Listening				
10. Communicating Through Evolving Media		✓	✓	✓
11. Mathematical				
12. Computer Applications	✓✓	✓	✓	✓
13. Teamwork and Interpersonal			✓	
14. Leadership and Assertiveness				
15. Conflict Management				
16. Decision Making	✓✓✓	✓✓		✓✓
17. Research	✓✓	✓	✓	✓
18. Critical Thinking			✓	✓
19. Responsible Risk Taking				
20. Creative Thinking and Visioning				
Pre-Requisites				

(continued)

New Directions for Teaching and Learning • DOI: 10.1002/tl

Exhibit 8.3. (continued)

Semester 2: Winter Courses

Skills	AHSS 1140 Public Sector Management	ECS 1010 Infant Development	ECS 2000 Parent Child Relations	ECS 1030 Field Placement I	ECS 1020 Child and Family Nutrition
1. Personal Organization and Time Management	✓		✓	✓	
2. Responsibility	✓		✓		✓
3. Adaptability					
4. Problem Solving	✓		✓	✓	
5. Resource Management	✓		✓	✓	
6. Reading	✓	✓	✓	✓	✓
7. Writing	✓	✓	✓	✓	✓
8. Speaking		✓	✓	✓	
9. Listening	✓	✓	✓	✓	✓
10. Communicating Through Evolving Media			✓		
11. Mathematical			✓		
12. Computer Applications					
13. Teamwork and Interpersonal		✓		✓	
14. Leadership and Assertiveness					
15. Conflict Management		✓			
16. Decision Making	✓	✓		✓	✓
17. Research	✓	✓	✓	✓	
18. Critical Thinking	✓	✓		✓	✓
19. Responsible Risk Taking			✓		
20. Creative Thinking and Visioning	✓			✓	
Pre-Requisites					

four full semesters in the workplace. This practical element provides reinforcement of the theoretical concepts introduced in the classroom.

Courses. To illustrate specific examples of integrating theory and practice, we shall provide an overview of three individual courses: first an elective for all programs, then two from the justice program. The first is the Science of Everyday Life, a first-year science course for nonscience majors. The second is the third-year course Canadian Social Problems, and the final course to be discussed is the fourth-year capstone course Transition to Work.

The Science of Everyday Life course integrates theory and practice into the examination of the ordinary. For example, organic chemistry is taught by delving into the process of cooking, changing on-hand ingredients into something different. Another component of the course is to critically examine how science is used or misused in the media.

The calendar description of the second course, Canadian Social Problems, reads: "Students critically examine Canadian social problems using a variety of sociological theories including Symbolic Interactionism, Conflict Theory, Feminism and Structural Functionalism. Topics studied include poverty and inequality, crime and deviance, drugs and addictions, ethnocentrism and racism, mental and physical illness, work and unemployment and gender issues. Particular emphasis is placed on a theoretical critique of social responses to these topics."

One of the unique elements of this course is the practical portion, where students go on a "street walk" or, as the course describes the field trip, to "observe social problems 'in-situ.'" This experience takes place at night in downtown Toronto, where students can see the nightlife of a cosmopolitan city for themselves. When students return to the classroom they are asked to write a paper reflecting on the experience and its relation to their own practice as human service workers.

The third course, Transition to Work, attempts to bring together all the elements of theory and practice learned within the program. Reflecting on education and work experience, each student compiles a *Bases of Competence* skills portfolio illustrating experience in each of the identified skills. The skills portfolio is like an artist's portfolio containing the artist's best drawings, paintings, and other original material. Each portfolio contains a personal mission statement, an intellectual autobiography, résumés in alternative formats, sample cover letters, a record of job interview experiences, and a presentation (with support material) of the development of skills in each of the four bases of competence: managing self, communicating, managing people and tasks, and mobilizing innovation and change (Evers, Rush, and Berdrow, 1998).

Lessons Learned

This exercise taught us a great deal. While the process was quite lengthy it did, we feel, produce an innovative and rigorous curriculum. One of the most useful aspects of the committee was extending membership across programs. This approach allowed for scrutiny and input from outside the discipline of the course under discussion. The outcome was twofold; although the length of curriculum review time was considerably increased, the end result was a tighter course with measurable learning objectives and consistency across programs.

Most of the difficulties we encountered derived from the parent institutional curriculum approval committees. Each committee needed to come to terms with the nature of and our intentions for the curriculum. For example, Guelph needed to accept the applied nature of content, whereas Humber needed to accept the substantive content in experiential learnings. We accomplished acceptance by going to committee meetings and answering questions until they were satisfied.

Another successful exercise involved organizing a full-day retreat for faculty who would be teaching the courses. We explained how we built the curriculum and why. In addition, because the instructors at Guelph-Humber are from both parent institutions and include sessional lecturers, we created opportunities to build community among faculty. Feedback showed that the faculty appreciated the event.

Conclusion

Now that the development of the curriculum for the first six programs at the University of Guelph-Humber is complete, the next step is to assess its effectiveness. This step began in winter 2007 with an online survey of the first set of students to graduate along with in-course students. Overall the feedback from students has been very positive, particularly in the area of skill development. Currently the data from the survey are being reviewed by university administration.

To conclude, we found that the process we undertook does actually work; however, it requires a lot of patience, time, supportive senior administration, and active program champions. More importantly we found that the use of learning objectives—knowledge, skills, and values—enhanced the process of curriculum development. It facilitated the examination of course content, course readings, assignments, and evaluation tools used in the course. Learning objectives focus course development on the learners—our students.

Although the curriculum development process for G-H has been fraught with administrative and cultural hurdles, the experience has also been very worthwhile. Learning is just as valuable to us as it is to our students. The process of merging two cultures and two sets of institutional policies has stretched our own skills of listening, problem solving, creative thinking, and visioning. Examining the procedures and practices of other experts encouraged us to reexamine our own methods and in turn strengthen our performance. One rewarding outcome from this exercise was the forging and strengthening of collegial relationships. Drawing on these reciprocal relationships has enhanced other projects we have undertaken.

New Directions for Teaching and Learning • DOI: 10.1002/tl

References

Evers, F. T., Rush, J. C., and Berdrow, I. *The Bases of Competence: Skills for Lifelong Learning and Employability.* San Francisco: Jossey-Bass, 1998.

Humber Institute of Technology and Advanced Learning. *Generic/Employability Skills.* Toronto, Ont.: Humber Institute of Technology and Advanced Learning, 2006.

University of Guelph. *Undergraduate Calendar: Learning Objectives.* Guelph, Ont.: University of Guelph, 2006. Retrieved from www.uoguelph.ca/registrar/calendars/undergraduate/current/c02/c02-learningobjectives.shtml.

FREDERICK EVERS *is a professor in sociology and the interim director of teaching support services at the University of Guelph. He is also a 3M teaching fellow.*

JANET WOLSTENHOLME *is an educational development associate at teaching support services at the University of Guelph. She also teaches at the University of Guelph-Humber.*

New Directions for Teaching and Learning • DOI: 10.1002/tl

9

This chapter provides an overview of externally generated program-level learning outcomes and an integrated and stage-specific framework for redeveloping learning-centered curricula in higher education contexts.

Supporting the Implementation of Externally Generated Learning Outcomes and Learning-Centered Curriculum Development: An Integrated Framework

Harry Hubball, Neil Gold, Joy Mighty, Judy Britnell

Higher education reform on an international scale is having a profound impact on organizations and institutions where there are now mandates and requirements to implement explicit learning outcomes and assessment policies for all undergraduate curricula (Bergen Communique, 2005; Bresciani, 2006; Hubball and Burt, 2004; Hubball and Gold, 2007; OCAV Report, 2005). Internationally, program-level outcomes are not only linked to government funding but are also used to facilitate credit transfers, admission to graduate programs, and accreditation of professional programs. In Canada education is a joint jurisdiction between provincial and federal governments, with the latter being primarily responsible for funding research in higher education. In the absence of a national accreditation process for university programs, quality assurance measures—particularly those centered around program-level learning outcomes—vary considerably from one province to the next.

The authors would like to express their thanks to educational developers, curriculum leaders, and faculty members in Ontario, especially at the University of Windsor and the Joint Working Group for Teaching and Learning, for their curricular contributions.

As previously argued (in Chapter One), program-level learning outcomes are a central component of learning-centered curricula. Once established (whether provincially, institutionally, or programmatically), they require careful integration and alignment to be effectively implemented. Localized development can be a major undertaking for most institutions and academic units. Addressing critical issues such as "how can learning outcomes be effectively implemented in our program?" and "how do we actually know that students are able to demonstrate these outcomes on completion of our degree program?" present significant challenges for many faculty members and administrators—the magnitude of which may well be an outright deterrent for some considering such a venture (Drummond, Nixon, and Wiltshire, 1998; Shavelson and Huang, 2003; Schneider and Shoenberg, 1999).

This chapter provides an overview of one Canadian provincially initiated curriculum reform effort in which several generic learning outcomes were established. It also presents a flexible, practical, and integrated framework for the development, implementation, and evaluation of program-level learning outcomes in undergraduate curricula contexts. When learning outcomes are externally mandated (or strongly encouraged), it is important that institutions have effective road maps for their implementation. Guiding principles and comprehensive strategies are provided here from critical lessons learned from the experience.

Provincial-Level Learning Outcomes: Building Capacity

In the summer of 2004, the government of Ontario established a commission to review the state of higher education. The commission's report emphasized the need to make explicit processes for ensuring quality and recommended that every university in Ontario should implement the National Survey for Student Engagement (see http://nsse.iub.edu; Rae, 2005). Later that year the Council of Ontario Universities (COU)—the organization of executive heads of Ontario's publicly assisted universities—proactively established its own task force made up of members of one of its subgroups, the Ontario Council of Academic Vice-Presidents (OCAV), to develop "Guidelines for University Undergraduate Degree Level Expectations" (UDLEs) to serve as a framework for describing expectations of attributes and performance by graduates of universities in Ontario (OCAV, 2005). The UDLEs consist of the following six generic categories of intellectual and creative development of graduates:

- Depth of knowledge
- Knowledge of methodologies
- Application of knowledge
- Communication skills
- Awareness of limits of knowledge
- Autonomy and professional capacity

NEW DIRECTIONS FOR TEACHING AND LEARNING • DOI: 10.1002/tl

The guidelines provide a short description of the minimum levels of performance that graduates of both honors and general degrees are expected to demonstrate for each attribute. Quality assurance measures in higher education are, however, not new to Ontario. In 1996, the COU established guidelines for the conduct of periodic quality reviews of undergraduate programs and committed to a system of regular audits of the Ontario universities' policies and procedures for these reviews. The body responsible for performing the audits is OCAV, operating through its Undergraduate Program Review Audit Committee (UPRAC). UPRAC audits provide institutions with valuable and objective advice on how they might take steps to improve their processes, but at the same time the audit process preserves the principles of university self-regulation and autonomy. The process includes three key components: self-study, peer review, and a judgment by the auditors about the quality of new and existing programs (OCAV, 2006). In 2005, the COU endorsed OCAV's "Guidelines for University Undergraduate Degree Level Expectations" (UDLEs), and universities agreed to use these guidelines in explicitly articulating their own undergraduate degree-level expectations based on their unique institutional values and goals and to develop policies for incorporating them into their program review processes by June 2008.

Implementing the initiative. In November 2005 OCAV invited academic leaders, including vice presidents, deans, chairs, members of standards committees, educational developers, and others engaged in program and curriculum development to participate in a full-day workshop to discuss the UDLEs and explore their implications for enhancing curricula. Following that workshop, OCAV and educational developers established a Joint Working Group on Teaching and Learning to identify strategic approaches, including regional workshops, for assisting universities in incorporating the UDLEs framework into their curricula. The workshops focused on building capacity for institutional curricula reform centered on student learning outcomes and objectives. Specifically the workshops enabled participants to identify, discuss, and align institutional graduate attributes with the provincial UDLEs. Furthermore, various curriculum development, implementation, and evaluation models were examined in which participants were required to develop action plan priorities (such as what, why, who, when, and how) for their respective institutions.

Coordinating the initiative. The OCAV Joint Working Group on Teaching and Learning is currently gathering data to monitor and guide institutional progress towards implementing UDLEs. A newly formed network of curriculum leaders serves as valuable support to provide workshops, resources, scholarly activities, and best-practice examples of integrating UDLEs into undergraduate degree programs. In particular, this initiative has provided an opportunity for a new coalition between educational developers and academic leaders to enhance the quality of teaching and learning in Ontario's higher education system.

An Integrated Framework for Developing, Implementing, and Evaluating Learning-Centered Curricula

Developing, implementing, and evaluating learning-centered curricula are complex, multifaceted, and iterative processes that cannot be treated as discrete and linear entities to suit all academic settings, but rather must be carefully integrated to meet the diverse needs and circumstances of undergraduate program contexts (Fullan, 2001; Green and Kreuter, 1999; Kotter, 1996). The following framework has been applied successfully in a variety of settings (Hubball and Burt, 2004; Albon and Hubball, 2004; Hubball and Burt, 2006; Hubball and Poole, 2004). It takes context into account and integrates comprehensive strategies for learning-centered curricula. Essentially this framework provides (1) a benchmark for an analysis of needs to determine the current status of curriculum within an academic unit, (2) guidelines for direction and progression in the curriculum redesign process, and (3) strategies for implementation and the scholarship of curriculum practice (SoCP).

Action research methodology is central to this integrated framework and SoCP (see Figure 9.1). Action research methodology invites curriculum leaders to consider which research questions are important and provides authentic data to reflect on and to initiate changes to the effectiveness of

Figure 9.1. Implications of an Integrated Framework for Developing, Implementing, and Evaluating Learning-Centered Curricula

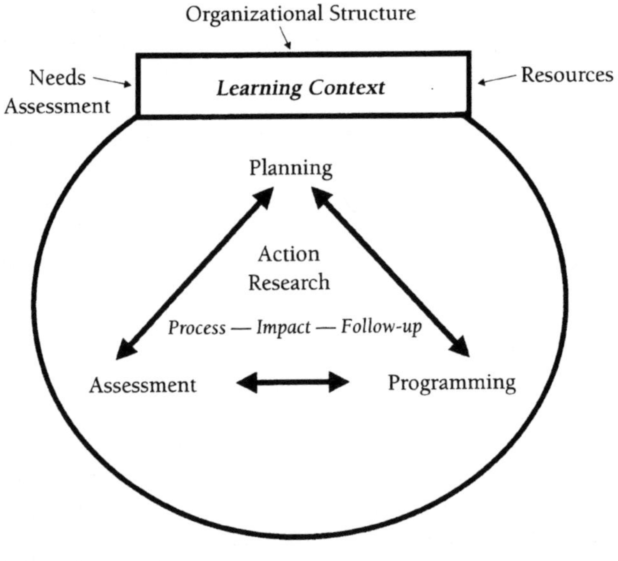

Source: Hubball and Burt, 2004.

NEW DIRECTIONS FOR TEACHING AND LEARNING • DOI: 10.1002/tl

program processes and outcomes (Bullough and Pinnegar, 2001; Gold, 1997; Thompson, 1996; Wolf, Hill and Evers, 2006).

Program Development and Implementation

Learning context strategies. This critical component of learning-centered curricula refers to key implementation initiatives, such as critical motivational factors for curriculum change, learning outcomes education, adequate support, leadership qualities, teamwork, representative input, responsiveness, incentives, sources of reward, and stage-specific curriculum support strategies. These initiatives empower the learning community, collectively and individually, to engage in the ongoing process of implementing progressive learning-centered curricula (Barab and Duffy, 2000; Cox and Richlin, 2004; Gold, 1997; Knight and Trowler, 2000). For example, in addition to understanding the unique context of a university and those situational factors in which academic units operate, it is important to recognize a unit's current readiness, stage, and progression with curricular reform.

Planning strategies. These refer to the development of global (overall curriculum) and specific (program-specialization) learning outcomes—such as acquisition, application, and integration of knowledge; research skills, including the ability to define problems and access, retrieve, and evaluate information; critical thinking and problem solving; proficient literacy and numeracy skills; responsible use of ethical principles; effective leadership, communication, and interpersonal skills. Learning outcomes, in part, drive the curricula, teaching, and learning process (Baird, 1996; Lockhart and Borland, 2001).

Assessment strategies. These refer to the development of a range of methods (such as capstone projects, portfolios, student presentations, and exams) and procedures used to assess and evaluate student learning and curriculum effectiveness—in terms of processes, impact, and outcomes (Brown, Bull, and Pendlebury, 1997; Green and Kreuter, 1999; Shavelson and Huang, 2003).

Programming strategies. These strategies inform the development and integration (both vertical and horizontal) of diverse learning experiences. They include interdisciplinary or core learning modules, intraprogram specialization modules, and individual course work modules—from learning technologies, problem-based learning, and lectures to independent study and field experiences—in which students can acquire, integrate, and apply knowledge in diverse settings (Poindexter, 2003).

Program Evaluation

The following program evaluation framework provides a broad and long perspective through which to investigate learning context, process, impact, and follow-up program evaluations (Fullan, 2001; Green and Kreuter, 1999; Kreber and Brook, 2001; Mills, 2000; Owen, Fletcher, and Richards, 2001; Priest, 2001).

New Directions for Teaching and Learning • DOI: 10.1002/tl

Learning context evaluations. These evaluations address key issues such as the intended audience for the evaluation, the objectives of the evaluation, and available resources to conduct specified evaluation projects. For example, learning context evaluations might include comprehensive data-gathering strategies for various stakeholder groups, researching relevant literature sources pertaining to learning outcomes in higher education, assessing perceived needs about program processes and outcomes, assessing critical factors in the development of localized learning outcomes, evaluating program feasibility issues, examining program cost-benefit issues, or investigating issues around learning outcomes and student recruitment. What needs to be improved and why and how?

Process evaluations. These focus on periodic assessments of issues of importance that arise throughout the program (formative evaluations). For example, to what extent are learning outcomes made explicitly clear to students? How do students best achieve learning outcomes? To what extent do learning experiences integrate learning outcomes? To what extent are learning outcomes reflected in course syllabi and program-level documentations? What are the strengths and weaknesses of program learning experiences? To what extent are learning context, planning, assessment, and programming strategies integrated with learning outcomes at key stages of a four-year program? What needs to be improved and why and how?

Impact evaluations. These focus on issues of importance that occur as a result of a program (or summative) evaluation. For example, what sorts of learning outcomes actually occurred as a result of this program? How do students demonstrate learning outcomes? To what extent does the program meet, surpass, or fall short of the identified learning outcomes, and why and how? What needs to be improved in terms of learning outcomes and program implementation? What needs to be improved and why and how?

Follow-up evaluations. These focus on issues of importance arising from the longer-term impact of a program (several months or a year later). For example, as a student reflects on the program and learning outcomes, what does he or she remember and value most? Generally speaking, to whom and to what extent, if at all, did the learning outcomes make any difference? If at all, how did the program contribute to the student's development? If at all, can specific examples be provided about applications of learning outcomes to other academic activities? What were alternative or unintended outcomes from this program?

The framework shown in Figure 9.1 therefore takes into account context and integrates comprehensive strategies for the development, implementation, and evaluation of learning-centered curricula. Academic units, however, face considerable learning context challenges (such as existing academic workload stress, a tradition of low priority for curriculum leadership and contributions in tenure and promotion processes, curriculum fatigue, and lack of localized expertise in the scholarship of curriculum practice) for developing, implementing, and evaluating learning-centered curricula. Thus, considering curriculum revision as a staged process of transition that requires a period of significant and incremental adaptation rather than radical and abrupt change helps to alleviate faculty anxiety or resistance (Hubball and Burt, 2004; Kupperschmidt and Burns, 1997). Typically academic units progress through cyclical and iterative stages of learning-centered curriculum reform: for example, a pre-awareness stage (curriculum reform is neither on the agenda nor a priority at all at this point); an awareness stage (awareness of groundswell of curricular reform in alternative settings, though no real energy or resources committed to curriculum change); an initiative stage (interest in and commitment to curriculum reform, initiate chair and key personnel to spearhead process); a mobilization stage (mobilize and empower learning community for curriculum reform, establish curriculum committee and subcommittee working groups for strategic planning); an action plan stage (buy-in readiness and integration of responsive outcomes, assessment strategies, and learning modules developed); and a practice stage (ongoing systematic analysis, refinement, further development, and dissemination).

Stage-Specific Support Strategies for Implementing Learning-Centered Curricula

Various strategies from the integrated framework discussed earlier have been useful in assisting academic units to progress through the stages of learning-centered curriculum reform. Generally learning context strategies are more important for developing a learning community and creating a critical mass to address issues of learning-centered curricula during the awareness, initiative, and mobilization stages, whereas emphases on program development and evaluation strategies tend to be more relevant during the overlapping mobilization, action plan, and practice stages of curriculum reform. The following stage-specific curriculum support strategies have been particularly useful for assisting academic units to progress through each of the iterative and cyclical stages of learning-centered curricula reform.

From Pre-awareness Stage to Awareness Stage. In the early stages it is useful to encourage all stakeholders in the learning community to identify internal and external motivation (contextual) factors for curriculum reform (via surveys, discussion forums, and meetings, for example) and to expose the learning community to a wide range of resources, guest speakers, and current literature pertaining to learning-centered curricula and best practices. These may include accreditation issues or government-mandated educational reforms.

From Awareness Stage to Initiative Stage. It is useful to build on the above strategies with a view to identifying an appropriate and potential curriculum leader or chairperson who could mobilize stakeholders through open dialogue and various communications and spearhead the redesign and implementation of a learning-centered curriculum. To ensure that the curriculum redesign process is grounded in pedagogical research and best practices for program development, implementation, and evaluation in higher education, the curriculum chair might seek the assistance of an external consultant with appropriate expertise in the scholarship of curriculum practice.

From Initiative Stage to Mobilization Stage. Typically university faculties and academic units embrace several subdisciplines, each with its own distinct subculture and perspective of the main discipline. Thus, from initiative to mobilization stages, it is useful to build on the above strategies and to engage and mobilize a critical mass, collectively and through disciplinary streams, in open dialogue and needs analysis pertaining to the curriculum reform process. This approach is particularly effective through town hall meetings (namely, discussion forums about curriculum issues for faculty, administrators, students, and professionals in the field), notice board information about ongoing issues and progress with curriculum reform process, individual and focus group interviews with faculty members, e-mail surveys and consultation with student and professional groups, and faculty development workshops on issues related to learning-centered curricula. These are excellent networking opportunities for identifying and recruiting potential curriculum team leaders who could mobilize personnel in subdisciplinary specializations.

From Mobilization Stage to Action Plan Stage. To ensure a well-designed and cohesive program among various subdisciplines requires an overall shared vision and model of curriculum with specific attention to learning outcomes and vertical and horizontal curriculum integration. Vertical integration refers to course work that progressively builds on previous course work with each subsequent year of the program (from the first to the fourth year), whereas horizontal integration refers to interrelated courses as a student progresses through each specific year of a program (Albon and Hubball, 2004; Beaudry and Schaub, 1998; Hubball and Burt, forthcoming; Lockhart and Borland, 2001; Raman-Wilms, 2001). Vertical integration can be addressed by organizing faculty members into specific groupings to identify and disseminate examples of innovative course design and best teaching practices within subspecializations. In addition, subdisciplinary specializations should be challenged to develop flexible, progressively challenging, and responsive course work (throughout years one to four of the program) in order to align and integrate learning outcomes with learning experiences and assessment strategies (Purkerson Hammer and Paulsen, 2001). Horizontal curriculum integration is best developed initially by the chair and curriculum team leaders in order to ensure that specifically designed courses (such as specific case-based, problem-based, project-based portfolio development and field placement learning modules courses) provide unique opportunities for students to apply and integrate learning outcomes and course work experiences from the individual disciplinary streams to the solving of progressively challenging multidisciplinary cases and problems throughout each year of the curriculum. It is important to emphasize that learning-centered curricula should not be overloaded, horizontally or vertically, with rigid

NEW DIRECTIONS FOR TEACHING AND LEARNING • DOI: 10.1002/tl

course modules. Rather, undergraduate programs require adequate flexibility to be able to respond to and provide cutting-edge learning experiences that originate from local and societal issues.

From Action Plan Stage to Practice Stage. In order to progress from the action plan stage to practice stage, academic units need to attend to all previous stage-specific strategies, as well as identify and disseminate best practices (such as innovative and integrated course work experiences) across the whole curriculum. Furthermore, a program evaluation team should be mobilized in preparation to address relevant research questions, gather appropriate data, and disseminate progress, critical challenges, and plans for ongoing refinements and investigations within the whole curriculum and subspecializations. External assistance may be useful for action research methodologies and the scholarship of curriculum practice.

Exhibit 9.1 indicates critical lessons learned by the authors in their various experiences in implementing curricular reform.

Exhibit 9.1. Critical Lessons Learned

- Accreditation was the single biggest factor to influence the development, implementation, and evaluation of learning-centered curricula.
- Strong and adequately supported curriculum leadership is required, with the ability to engage the *whole* learning community (including a critical mass within the subdisciplines) through open dialogue and other varied communications such as town hall meetings, faculty retreats, faculty meetings, notice boards, and web site displays.
- Learning outcomes that are predetermined and imposed from the top down typically meet greater resistance than localized "bottom-up" versions, which often produce similar and easily aligned outcomes.
- Guest speakers and external consultants with expertise in the scholarship of curriculum practice in higher education can provide broader perspectives and best-practice examples to assist the context-specific development, implementation, and evaluation of learning-centered curricula.
- Development, implementation, and evaluation of learning-centered curricula is a complex labor-intensive and relational process (much like effective teaching, but on a much broader scale), therefore realistic time frames and adequate curriculum and faculty development support structures should be established in order for academic units to progress successfully through the cyclical and iterative stage-specific processes of learning-centered curricula reform. (For example, the eight-month Faculty Certificate Program began in 1998 at the University of British Columbia and has enabled individuals and groups of faculty members, through various assignments, workshops, and one-to-one tutorials, to focus on leadership issues pertaining to the scholarship of curriculum and pedagogical practice.)
- The considerable time and effort required, individually and collectively, to successfully develop, implement, and evaluate learning-centered curricula require equal consideration for the varied contributions from faculty members within academic units in the realms of workload expectations, provisions for curriculum grant funding and award structures, and credit toward tenure and promotion processes.
- Provide additional support for select groups with early potential who are likely to offer case examples and to champion innovation, leadership, and integration of learning-centered curricula.
- Development, implementation, and evaluation of learning-centered curricula is an individual and social contextual process.

Institutional Application

Following its establishment of the list of the University of Windsor graduate characteristics and alignment of these with provincially mandated degree-level expectations, the university undertook a comprehensive institution-wide curriculum reform effort. In order to honor the diverse needs and circumstances of students, faculty, and the wider setting of university operations, an institutional visioning process sought to engage the campus community through open dialogue and various interactive forums to collectively define, develop, and implement notions of a learning-centered campus (University of Windsor Senate, 2006). Integral to the institutional visioning process, all academic units on campus were challenged to reexamine their curricula and pedagogical practices in the context of program-level learning outcomes, the University of Windsor graduate characteristics, and the provincial UDLEs.

Part of the community engagement process was to invite visiting scholars with various perspectives and research and practical expertise in issues of curriculum development and pedagogy in higher education. For example, a curriculum consultant was invited to spend an intensive three-day workshop and consultation series with deans, heads, senate, curricula leaders, academic units, and individual faculty members. The consultant's role was not to tell curricular committees how to redesign their curricula but rather to understand the various learning contexts and to engage faculty with flexible frameworks and strategic approaches for developing, implementing, and evaluating learning-centered curricula. Typically this involved a series of introductory program-specific workshops and consultations that focused on the context for learning-centered curriculum reform in higher education (local and global initiatives), identifying shared program-level values and student learning-outcomes, developing cutting-edge and progressive learning experiences for students at strategic phases of the specified undergraduate program, and critical ways of judging the quality and effectiveness of the specified undergraduate program.

Three specific faculties on campus were targeted for special attention and additional workshop and consultancy support over a one-year period in order to role-model and champion best practices at the institutional level. Context-specific issues emerged as these units progressed through various key stages of curriculum reform. Examples of more advanced workshops in these program-specific contexts focused on faculty learning communities' implications for program reform and curriculum leadership, program-level learning outcomes' implications for assessment and course design, program-level learning outcomes' implications for diverse teaching and learning strategies, and program-level evaluation (action research and the scholarship of curriculum practice). Ongoing monitoring and specific consultations with each of these curriculum chairs tended to reinforce and connect context-specific change processes with scholarly approaches to curriculum practice. Finally, as part of a comprehensive institutional curriculum sup-

NEW DIRECTIONS FOR TEACHING AND LEARNING • DOI: 10.1002/tl

port initiative, five curriculum leaders from various faculties on campus were funded to develop further expertise in university curriculum and pedagogy by attending the eight-month Faculty Certificate Program on Teaching and Learning in Higher Education at the University of British Columbia.

Conclusion

Universities and academic units are increasingly being encouraged to develop, adopt, and implement program-level learning outcomes within undergraduate curricula. Learning-centered curricula take time, collective energy, and resources to fully implement. The extent to which the learning community (the campus) is empowered will have a significant effect on progress made through the various stages of implementing learning-centered curricula. Also significant is the commitment of adequate resources (such as necessary levels of support for committee chairs and curriculum leaders) and the power to influence people required during this process (such as appropriate leadership qualities, commitment, incentives, and ability of curricular leaders to mobilize faculty and students). Furthermore, despite well-coordinated, innovative, and strategic attempts to implement learning-centered curricula, it is unlikely to fully occur as intended due to the highly complex world of curriculum practice. It is not surprising, therefore, that inherent complexities in implementing learning-centered curricula can present significant pedagogical as well as implementation challenges for institutions and academic units in higher education. By implication, these challenges also extend to individual faculty who are required to reexamine their course design, assessment, and learning strategies in order to meet the objectives of a learning-centered curriculum.

This chapter provides a useful integrated and stage-specific framework for implementing learning outcomes in various higher education contexts, as well as highlighting critical contributions for the scholarship of curriculum practice toward enhancing student learning. This framework takes context into account and integrates comprehensive strategies to assist academic units with redesigning and implementing learning-centered curricula.

References

Albon, S., and Hubball, H. T. "Course Design in Pharmaceutical Sciences: A Learning-Centred Approach." *American Journal of Pharmaceutical Education,* 2004, *68*(5).
Baird, L. L. "Documenting Student Outcomes in Graduate and Professional Programs." In A. E. Bilder and C. F. Conrad (eds.), *Challenges in Assessing Outcomes in Graduate and Professional Education.* New Directions for Institutional Research, no. 92. San Francisco: Jossey-Bass, 1996.
Barab, S. A., and Duffy, T. "From Practice Fields to Communities of Practice." In D. Jonassen and S. M. Land (eds.), *Theoretical Foundations of Learning Environments.* Mahwah, N.J.: Erlbaum, 2000.
Beaudry, M. L., and Schaub, T. "The Learning-Centred Syllabus." *The Teaching Professor,* 1998, *12*(2), 5.

Bergen Communique. "The European Higher Education Area: Achieving the Goals." Communique of the Conference of European Ministers Responsible for Higher Education: The Bologna Process, Bergen, May 2005.

Bresciani, M. J. *Outcomes-Based Academic and Co-curricular Program Review.* Sterling, Va.: Stylus, 2006.

Brown, G., Bull, J., and Pendlebury, M. *Assessing Student Learning in Higher Education.* London: Routledge, 1997.

Bullough, R., and Pinnegar, S. "Guidelines for Quality in Autobiographical Forms of Self-Study Research." *Educational Researcher,* 2001, *30*(3), 13–21.

Cox, M., and Richlin, L. (Eds.). *Building Faculty Learning Communities.* New Directions for Teaching and Learning, no. 97. San Francisco: Jossey-Bass, 2004.

Drummond, I., Nixon, I., and Wiltshire, J. "Personal Transferable Skills in Higher Education: The Problems of Implementing Good Practice." *Quality Assurance in Education,* 1998, *6*(1), 44–58.

Fullan, M. G. *The New Meaning of Educational Change.* (3rd ed.) New York: Teachers College, Columbia University, 2001.

Gold, P. "Faculty Collaboration for a New Curriculum." *Liberal Education,* 1997, *83*(1), 46–49.

Green, L. W., and Kreuter, M. *Health Promotion Planning: An Educational and Ecological Approach.* Palo Alto, Calif.: Mayfield, 1999.

Hubball, H. T., and Burt, H. D. "An Integrated Approach to Developing and Implementing Learning-Centred Curricula." *International Journal for Academic Development,* 2004, *9*(1), 51–65.

Hubball, H. T., and Burt, H. D. "Scholarship of Teaching and Learning: Theory-Practice Integration in Faculty Certificate Programs." *Innovative Higher Education,* 2006, *30*(5), 327–344.

Hubball, H. T., and Burt, H. D. "Learning Outcomes and Program-Level Evaluation in a Four-Year Undergraduate Pharmacy Curriculum." *American Journal of Pharmaceutical Education,* forthcoming.

Hubball, H. T., and Gold, N. "The Scholarship of Curriculum Practice and Undergraduate Program Reform: Theory Practice Integration." In D. Cox and L. Richlin (eds.), New Directions for Teaching and Learning, no. 97. San Francisco: Jossey-Bass, 2007.

Hubball, H. T., and Poole, G. "A Learning-Centred Course on University Teaching." *International Journal for Academic Development,* 2004, *8*(2), 11–24.

Knight, P. T., and Trowler, P. R. "Department-Level Cultures and the Improvement of Learning and Teaching." *Studies in Higher Education,* 2000, *25*(1), 69–83.

Kotter, J. P. *Leading Change.* Boston: Harvard Business School Press, 1996.

Kreber, C., and Brook, P. "Impact Evaluation of Educational Development Programs." *International Journal for Academic Development,* 2001, *6*(2), 96–108.

Kupperschmidt, B. R., and Burns, P. "Curriculum Revision Isn't Just Change: It's Transition!" *Journal of Professional Nursing,* 1997, *13*(2), 90–98.

Lockhart, M., and Borland, K. W. "Critical Thinking Goals, Outcomes, and Pedagogy in Senior Capstone Courses." *Journal of Faculty Development,* 2001, *18*(1), 19–25.

Mills, G. E. *Action Research: A Guide for the Teacher Researcher.* Upper Saddle River, N.J.: Merrill Prentice Hall, 2000.

OCAV. "Undergraduate Program Review Audit Committee (UPRAC) Review and Audit Guidelines." 2006. www.cou.on.ca/_bin/affiliates/associations/upracmain.cfm.

OCAV. "Guidelines for University Undergraduate Degree-Level Expectations." 2005. www.cou.on.ca/content/objects/Undergrad%20Degree%20Expectations%20FINALen.pdf.

OCAV Report. Working Group on University Undergraduate Degree-Level Expectations. Ontario Council of Academic Vice-Presidents, Oct. 24, 2005. http://72.14.253.104/search?q=cache:gsQ9IKN9NDMJ:www.uwo.ca/univsec/handbook/general/OCAV_

Guidelines_2005.pdf+Ontario+Council+of+Academic+Vice-Presidents&hl=en&gl=ca&ct=clnk&cd=3.

Owen, J., Fletcher, C., and Richards, K. "Evaluating a School-Based Experiential Personal Development Course." *Horizons,* 2001, *16,* 27–31.

Poindexter, S. "Holistic Learning." *Change,* Jan.–Feb. 2003, pp. 25–30.

Priest, S. "A Program Evaluation Primer." *Journal of Experiential Education,* 2001, 24(1), 34–40.

Purkerson Hammer, D., and Paulsen, S. M. "Strategies and Processes to Design an Integrated, Longitudinal Professional Skills Development Course Sequence." *American Journal of Pharmaceutical Education,* 2001, *65,* 77–85.

Rae, R. *The Ontario Post-secondary Review.* 2005. www.gov.on.ca.

Raman-Wilms, L. "Innovative Enabling Strategies in Self-Directed, Problem-Based Therapeutics: Enhancing Student Preparedness for Pharmaceutical Care Practice." *American Journal of Pharmaceutical Education,* 2001, *65,* 56–64.

Schneider, C. G., and Shoenberg, R. "Habits Hard to Break: How Persistent Features of Campus Life Frustrate Curricular Reform." *Change,* Mar.–Apr. 1999, pp. 30–35.

Shavelson, R., and Huang, L. "Responding Responsibly to the Frenzy to Assess Learning in Higher Education." *Change,* Jan.–Feb. 2003, pp. 11–18.

Thompson, S. "How Action Research Can Put Teachers and Parents on the Same Team." *Educational Horizons,* 1996, 74(2), 70–76.

University of Windsor Senate. "Definition of 'Learning-Centred' at the University of Windsor." 2006. www.uwindsor.ca/units/pac/learningcentred.nsf/inToc/7BB850CA3094BADB852570A6006568A8.

Wolf, P., Hill, A., and Evers, F. *A Handbook for Curriculum Assessment.* Guelph, Ont.: University of Guelph, 2006.

HARRY HUBBALL *is associate professor in the Department of Curriculum Studies at the University of British Columbia. He is a 3M National Teaching Fellow and cochair of the Faculty Certificate Program on Teaching and Learning in Higher Education at the University of British Columbia.*

NEIL GOLD *is academic vice president and provost at the University of Windsor, Canada, and a member of the Ontario Council of Academic Vice-Presidents.*

JOY MIGHTY *is director of the Centre for Teaching and Learning and professor in Organizational Behaviour in the School of Business at Queen's University. An award-winning teacher, she is also president of the Society for Teaching and Learning in Higher Education.*

JUDY BRITNELL *is director of the Learning and Teaching Office at Ryerson University, Toronto, and a member of the Joint Working Group for Teaching and Learning.*

NEW DIRECTIONS FOR TEACHING AND LEARNING • DOI: 10.1002/tl

10

This chapter argues that increased curriculum assessment and development activities are both essential and inevitable. The question is how best to support them?

Supporting Curriculum Assessment and Development: Implications for the Faculty Role and Institutional Support

Julia Christensen Hughes

As suggested elsewhere in this volume, growing interest in curriculum assessment and development in higher education is the result of a number of external and internal factors. External factors include increasing government interest in quality assurance, accessibility, and degree completion rates; growing recognition of the important role university graduates play in fueling innovation, economic growth, and contributing to the quality of society; and the desire for enhanced interinstitutional cooperation in the form of degree credit transfer. Other external influences include granting councils, accrediting bodies, employers, and parents, many of whom are increasingly advocating for the enhanced integration of disciplinary knowledge with skill development and practical application at all levels of university education (bachelor's, master's, and doctoral).

Internal influences include growing interest on the part of faculty, educational developers, students, and administrators in improving the quality and relevance of the higher education experience—at institutional, faculty or college, and program or department levels—in particular through the development of learning-centered curricula, interdisciplinary programs, and constructivist pedagogical approaches. Growing student numbers (including adult learners wishing to learn by distance) and declining budgets have also prompted interest in curriculum development, though of another

NEW DIRECTIONS FOR TEACHING AND LEARNING, no. 112, Winter 2007 © Wiley Periodicals, Inc.
Published online in Wiley InterScience (www.interscience.wiley.com) • DOI: 10.1002/tl.302

sort—determining how to maintain quality as class sizes swell and how to most effectively design courses for online environments. Given all of these influences and pressures, a growing level of interest in curriculum assessment and development appears to be both inevitable and essential.

The question then is, How can we best support curriculum assessment and development? By synthesizing the contributions from this volume, several important recommendations can be made. A number of chapters recognize the importance of developing a long-term vision consistent with the institution's or department's values and culture and inspired by a focus on student learning and constructivist pedagogical approaches. They also advocate using a collaborative, faculty-driven process facilitated by educational developers but involving all key stakeholders, in particular students. Doing so may be particularly helpful in creating a climate conducive to change, in which stakeholders' concerns are addressed and individuals come to perceive change as necessary. In addition, it is essential that credible faculty champions be identified, empowered, and supported and that clear and realistic time-lines be developed.

Several chapters here also suggest that the process must be data driven, supported by a scholarly (or an action-based research) approach to question posing, data gathering, analysis, and application. The importance of multiple data sources (students, faculty, and employers) is emphasized along with the importance of multiple data types (such as student work, surveys, focus groups, and interviews). A new concept has also been introduced—the scholarship of curriculum practice (SoCP)—which builds on the idea of a scholarly approach to curriculum practice by additionally involving dissemination of results and peer review.

Other chapters touch on the importance of effectively managing or bringing into alignment a number of institutional practices or systems that if left unchecked could potentially present considerable barriers to curriculum assessment, development, and implementation processes. Such systems include curricular approval processes; course assignment processes; and faculty training and development opportunities, selection processes, and reward systems.

Finally, several interesting frameworks and models are presented on the importance of, and methods for, identifying meaningful and appropriate program-level learning outcomes (the attributes of the ideal graduate), as well as mechanisms for ensuring their thoughtful integration across the curriculum and their alignment with course- and class-level learning and assessment activities.

In reflecting on all these recommendations, I am most struck by their implications for the faculty role. They imply, to begin with, that faculty must develop a significantly broader skill set and knowledge base than has traditionally been the case. Faculty must become adept at working in teams, facilitating change, project management, and facilitating learning, to name a few of the skills needed. They must also become knowledgeable about curricular assessment and development processes and learning-centered or con-

NEW DIRECTIONS FOR TEACHING AND LEARNING • DOI: 10.1002/tl

structivist pedagogical theory. This point has profound implications for the training and development of the future professoriate, which in turn has implications for the training, development, and resourcing of educational development professionals. Institutions must continue to invest in their faculty development offices and ensure that their educational developers are prepared to support faculty development and curricular assessment and development activities.

The implied changes to the faculty role also have implications for selection and reward processes. For example, candidates with experience leading a curricular reform process or implementing an innovative pedagogy may increasingly be preferred—or even required—in faculty selection decisions. In addition, given the inherent complexity and amount of time involved in curricular assessment and development processes, faculty who provide leadership for this work should be adequately compensated for doing so (through allocation of effort, recognition, and the like). In short, in order for this work to flourish, faculty development, selection, and reward processes must all become aligned. Otherwise potential faculty champions will be limited to those who are willing to pay a heavy personal price in support of a personally meaningful goal.

Another implication for the faculty role is the suggestion that faculty should adopt a scholarly approach in their service and teaching activities. This is a particularly important recommendation because it makes explicit the implicit: we in the professoriate may have lost sight of what it means to be a scholar. Perhaps as a result of the dichotomy between research and teaching, heavy workloads, or simply lack of critical awareness, many faculty appear to routinely make decisions in their teaching and service activities that are not evidence based (a standard they would not accept in their research activity). It has been suggested by some contributors in this volume that the attention being paid to curricular assessment and development activities may have a number of positive unintended consequences. Reminding faculty of the importance of fully being a scholar—by adopting a scholarly approach in all activities—may be one such outcome. Encouraging institutions to provide recognition and support for the scholarship of teaching and learning is another.

Finally, perhaps the most important implication of all is the changing faculty role with respect to course development and delivery. Until very recently most university faculty enjoyed a significant amount of freedom in deciding what and how to teach (the exception being professional programs, which have long been influenced by accrediting bodies). Some refer to this practice as academic freedom. Within this model, program-level learning outcomes were rarely articulated, course-level learning outcomes were few and focused primarily on what the students would "learn" with respect to disciplinary content, and there was little thought of integration with other courses. In other words, courses were treated more or less as islands unto themselves.

Curriculum assessment and development processes challenge this approach, emphasizing program- and course-level learning outcomes that

NEW DIRECTIONS FOR TEACHING AND LEARNING • DOI: 10.1002/tl

encompass knowledge, skills, and values domains, as well as their deliberate integration across the curriculum. The important point here is that in our exuberance for more thoughtful, planned, and effective curricula it is vital that we don't allow the pendulum to swing too far the other way. In other words, curriculum assessment and development should provide a *framework* or a curricular map—within which faculty may still exercise discretion over course content, learning activities, and assessments—not a manual in which all these issues are minutely detailed.

In conclusion, curricular assessment and development are exceedingly important activities that faculty will be increasingly expected to champion and support. This volume presents the reasons for this trend, frameworks for engaging in such processes, and lessons learned. It also identifies significant implications for the faculty role along with significant implications for institutional support.

JULIA CHRISTENSEN HUGHES, PhD, is chair of the Department of Business at the University of Guelph, in Ontario, former director of Teaching Support Services, and past president of the Society for Teaching and Learning in Higher Education (STLHE).

NEW DIRECTIONS FOR TEACHING AND LEARNING • DOI: 10.1002/tl

INDEX

Academic freedom, 109
Alberts, N., 76
Albon, S., 96, 100
Alignment, curriculum, 18–19
Altrichter, H., 10
Anderson, L., 34
Arts and sciences (ASCI) core, 59–67
Assessment, and faculty-level curricular evolution, 69–81
Assessment case study, 33–44

Baird, L. L., 9, 97
Ballard, B., 9
Barab, S. A., 8, 97
Baron, M. A., 8
Barr, R., 8, 24
Bath, D., 19
Beaudry, M. L., 100
Berdrow, I., 17, 85, 89
Biggs, J., 16, 27
Bisson, B., 74
Bloom, B., 34
Bondi, J., 7
Borland, K. W., 97, 100
Boyatzis, R., 77
Bresciani, M. J., 7, 9, 93
Brook, P., 97
Brown, G., 97
Bruner, J. S., 22
Bull, J., 97
Bullough, R., 10, 97
Burns, P., 8, 99
Burt, H. D., 8, 9, 93, 96, 99, 100

Change strategies, 23–24
Chickering, A., 24
Christie, P., 8
Clanchy, J., 9
Clark, S., 40
Continuous curriculum improvement, 33–44; evaluate, observe, and reflect element, 35–36; food science program background, 33–34, 35; independent learning as outcome, 41; learning fractal for, 34, 35–39, 40; learning objectives, teaching techniques, and evaluation techniques, 37–39; learning realms and learning objectives, 37; next steps for, 43–44;

as qualitative vs. quantitative, 40–41; self-assessment portfolios, 41; sustainability of, 41–43; tools for assessment, 35–36; transferability of, 43
Corbin, J., 10
Cox, M., 9, 97
Curricular evolution and assessment, faculty-level, 69–81; assessment and redesign processes, 75–76; capacity-building processes, 76–77; challenges in, 80; college life activities, 72; curricular evolution processes, 72–77; disciplinary minor, 72; integrated forum courses, 71; internships, 72; key ideas, 77–79; leadership stream, 71–72; learning outcomes, 70–71; learning portfolio, 72; outcomes courses, 71; sustaining process of, 79–80; visioning and strategic planning processes, 74–75. *See also* Curriculum evolution model
Curriculum assessment and development: faculty role in, 108–109; as framework, 110; growing interest in, 107–108
Curriculum change: course-level, 21; institutional-level, 22. *See also* Curriculum change, departmental-level
Curriculum change, departmental-level, 21–31; as consensus driven, 25–26; differentiation across disciplines, 29–30; embedded consultant for, 29; external review of, 28–29; factors encouraging, 25–30; faculty member roles, 30–31; grants program, 24–25, 31; and how students learn, 26–27; long-term vision role in, 25; as scholarly, 27–28; stability in personal for, 29; and team work among departments, 27
Curriculum development process, 83–90; courses, 89; learning objectives, 85–89; original programs, 83–84; lessons learned, 89–90
Curriculum evolution model, 16–20; alignment/coordination/development phase, 18–19; attributes, 19; development phase, 18; visioning phase, 16–18. *See also* Curricular evolution and assessment, faculty-level

111

faculty embarking on curriculum revisions and identifying and measuring student learning outcomes for undergraduate and graduate students.
ISBN: 07879-9721-2

TL108 **Developing Student Expertise and Community: Lessons from How People Learn**
Anthony J. Petrosino, Taylor Martin, Vanessa Svihla
This issue presents research from a collaboration among learning scientists, assessment experts, technologists, and subject-matter experts, with the goal of producing adaptive expertise in students. The model is based on the National Research Council book *How People Learn*. The chapters present case studies of working together to develop learning environments centered on challenge-based instruction. While the strategies and research come from engineering, they are applicable across disciplines to help students think about the process of problem solving.
ISBN: 07879-9574-6

TL107 **Exploring Research-Based Teaching**
Carolin Kreber
Investigates the wide scope research-based teaching, while focusing on two distinct forms. The first sees research-based teaching as student-focused, inquiry-based learning; students become generators of knowledge. The second perspective fixes the lens on teachers; the teaching is characterized by discipline-specific inquiry into the teaching process itself. Both methods have positive effects on student learning, and this volume explores research and case studies.
ISBN: 07879-9077-9

TL106 **Supplemental Instruction: New Visions for Empowering Student Learning**
Marion E. Stone, Glen Jacobs
Supplemental Instruction (SI) is an academic support model introduced over thirty years ago to help students be successful in difficult courses. SI teaches students how to learn via regularly scheduled, out-of-class collaborative sessions with other students. This volume both introduces the tenets of SI to beginners and brings those familiar up to speed with today's methods and the future directions. Includes case studies, how-to's, benefits to students and faculty, and more.
ISBN: 0-7879-8680-1

TL105 **A Laboratory for Public Scholarship and Democracy**
Rosa A. Eberly, Jeremy Cohen
Public scholarship has grown out of the scholarship-and-service model, but its end is democracy rather than volunteerism. The academy has intellectual and creative resources that can help build involved, democratic communities through public scholarship. Chapters present concepts, processes, and case studies from Penn State's experience with public scholarship.
ISBN: 0-7879-8530-9

TL104 **Spirituality in Higher Education**
Sherry L. Hoppe, Bruce W. Speck
With chapters by faculty and administrators, this book investigates the role of spirituality in educating the whole student while recognizing that how spirituality is viewed, taught, and experienced is intensely personal. The goal is not to prescribe a method for integrating spirituality but to offer options and perspectives. Readers will be reminded that the quest for truth and meaning, not the destination, is what is vitally important.
ISBN: 0-7879-8363-2

TL103   **Identity, Learning, and the Liberal Arts**
Ned Scott Laff
Argues that we must foster conversations between liberal studies and student development theory, because the skills inherent in liberal learning are the same skills used for personal development. Students need to experience core learning that truly influences their critical thinking skills, character development, and ethics. Educators need to design student learning encounters that develop these areas. This volume gives examples of how liberal arts education can be a healthy foundation for life skills.
ISBN: 0-7879-8333-0

TL102   **Advancing Faculty Learning Through Interdisciplinary Collaboration**
Elizabeth G. Creamer, Lisa R. Lattuca
Explores why stakeholders in higher education should refocus attention on collaboration as a form of faculty learning. Chapters give theoretical basis then practical case studies for collaboration's benefits in outreach, scholarship, and teaching. Also discusses impacts on education policy, faculty hiring and development, and assessment of collaborative work.
ISBN: 0-7879-8070-6

TL101   **Enhancing Learning with Laptops in the Classroom**
Linda B. Nilson, Barbara E. Weaver
This volume contains case studies—mostly from Clemson University's leading-edge laptop program—that address victories as well as glitches in teaching with laptop computers in the classroom. Disciplines using laptops include psychology, music, statistics, animal sciences, and humanities. The volume also advises faculty on making a laptop mandate successful at their university, with practical guidance for both pedagogy and student learning.
ISBN: 0-7879-8049-8

TL100   **Alternative Strategies for Evaluating Student Learning**
Michelle V. Achacoso, Marilla D. Svinicki
Teaching methods are adapting to the modern era, but innovation in assessment of student learning lags behind. This volume examines theory and practical examples of creative new methods of evaluation, including authentic testing, testing with multimedia, portfolios, group exams, visual synthesis, and performance-based testing. Also investigates improving students' ability to take and learn from tests, before and after.
ISBN: 0-7879-7970-8

TL99   **Addressing Faculty and Student Classroom Improprieties**
John M. Braxton, Alan E. Bayer
Covers the results of a large research study on occurrence and perceptions of classroom improprieties by both students and faculty. When classroom norms are violated, all parties in a classroom are affected, and teaching and learning suffer. The authors offer guidelines for both student and faculty classroom behavior and how institutions might implement those suggestions.
ISBN: 0-7879-7794-2

TL98   **Decoding the Disciplines: Helping Students Learn Disciplinary Ways of Thinking**
David Pace, Joan Middendorf
The Decoding the Disciplines model is a way to teach students the critical-thinking skills required to understand their specific discipline. Faculty define bottlenecks to learning, dissect the ways experts deal with the problematic issues, and invent ways to model experts' thinking for students. Chapters are

written by faculty in diverse fields who successfully used these methods and became involved in the scholarship of teaching and learning.
ISBN: 0-7879-7789-6

TL97   **Building Faculty Learning Communities**
Milton D. Cox, Laurie Richlin
A very effective way to address institutional challenges is a faculty learning community. FLCs are useful for preparing future faculty, reinvigorating senior faculty, and implementing new courses, curricula, or campus initiatives. The results of FLCs parallel those of student learning communities, such as retention, deeper learning, respect for others, and greater civic participation. This volume describes FLCs from a practitioner's perspective, with plenty of advice, wisdom, and lessons for starting your own FLC.
ISBN: 0-7879-7568-0

TL96   **Online Student Ratings of Instruction**
Trav D. Johnson, D. Lynn Sorenson
Many institutions are adopting Web-based student ratings of instruction, or are considering doing it, because online systems have the potential to save time and money among other benefits. But they also present a number of challenges. The authors of this volume have firsthand experience with electronic ratings of instruction. They identify the advantages, consider costs and benefits, explain their solutions, and provide recommendations on how to facilitate online ratings.
ISBN: 0-7879-7262-2

TL95   **Problem-Based Learning in the Information Age**
Dave S. Knowlton, David C. Sharp
Provides information about theories and practices associated with problem-based learning, a pedagogy that allows students to become more engaged in their own education by actively interpreting information. Today's professors are adopting problem-based learning across all disciplines to faciliate a broader, modern definition of what it means to learn. Authors provide practical experience about designing useful problems, creating conducive learning environments, facilitating students' activities, and assessing students' efforts at problem solving.
ISBN: 0-7879-7172-3

TL94   **Technology: Taking the Distance out of Learning**
Margit Misangyi Watts
This volume addresses the possibilities and challenges of computer technology in higher education. The contributors examine the pressures to use technology, the reasons not to, the benefits of it, the feeling of being a learner as well as a teacher, the role of distance education, and the place of computers in the modern world. Rather than discussing only specific successes or failures, this issue addresses computers as a new cultural symbol and begins meaningful conversations about technology in general and how it affects education in particular.
ISBN: 0-7879-6989-3

TL93   **Valuing and Supporting Undergraduate Research**
Joyce Kinkead
The authors gathered in this volume share a deep belief in the value of undergraduate research. Research helps students develop skills in problem

solving, critical thinking, and communication, and undergraduate researchers' work can contribute to an institution's quest to further knowledge and help meet societal challenges. Chapters provide an overview of undergraduate research, explore programs at different types of institutions, and offer suggestions on how faculty members can find ways to work with undergraduate researchers.
ISBN: 0-7879-6907-9

TL92   **The Importance of Physical Space in Creating Supportive Learning Environments**
Nancy Van Note Chism, Deborah J. Bickford
The lack of extensive dialogue on the importance of learning spaces in higher education environments prompted the essays in this volume. Chapter authors look at the topic of learning spaces from a variety of perspectives, elaborating on the relationship between physical space and learning, arguing for an expanded notion of the concept of learning spaces and furnishings, talking about the context within which decision making for learning spaces takes place, and discussing promising approaches to the renovation of old learning spaces and the construction of new ones.
ISBN: 0-7879-6344-5

TL91   **Assessment Strategies for the On-Line Class: From Theory to Practice**
Rebecca S. Anderson, John F. Bauer, Bruce W. Speck
Addresses the kinds of questions that instructors need to ask themselves as they begin to move at least part of their students' work to an on-line format. Presents an initial overview of the need for evaluating students' on-line work with the same care that instructors give to the work in hard-copy format. Helps guide instructors who are considering using on-line learning in conjunction with their regular classes, as well as those interested in going totally on-line.
ISBN: 0-7879-6343-7

TL90   **Scholarship in the Postmodern Era: New Venues, New Values, New Visions**
Kenneth J. Zahorski
A little over a decade ago, Ernest Boyer's *Scholarship Reconsidered* burst upon the academic scene, igniting a robust national conversation that maintains its vitality to this day. This volume aims at advancing that important conversation. Its first section focuses on the new settings and circumstances in which the act of scholarship is being played out; its second identifies and explores the fresh set of values currently informing today's scholarly practices; and its third looks to the future of scholarship, identifying trends, causative factors, and potentialities that promise to shape scholars and their scholarship in the new millennium.
ISBN: 0-7879-6293-7

TL89   **Applying the Science of Learning to University Teaching and Beyond**
Diane F. Halpern, Milton D. Hakel
Seeks to build on empirically validated learning activities to enhance what and how much is learned and how well and how long it is remembered. Demonstrates that the movement for a real science of learning—the application of scientific principles to the study of learning—has taken hold both under the controlled conditions of the laboratory and in the messy real-world settings where most of us go about the business of teaching and learning.
ISBN: 0-7879-5791-7

NEW DIRECTIONS FOR TEACHING AND LEARNING
Order Form
SUBSCRIPTIONS AND SINGLE ISSUES

DISCOUNTED BACK ISSUES:

Use this form to receive **20% off** *all back issues of New Directions for Teaching and Learning. All single issues priced at* **$23.20** *(normally $29.00).*

TITLE	ISSUE NO.	ISBN
_____	_____	_____
_____	_____	_____
_____	_____	_____

Call **888-378-2537** *or see mailing instructions below. When calling, mention the promotional code,* JB7ND, *to receive your discount.*

SUBSCRIPTIONS: *(1 year, 4 issues)*

☐ New Order   ☐ Renewal

U.S.	☐ Individual: $80	☐ Institutional: $195
Canada/Mexico	☐ Individual: $80	☐ Institutional: $235
All Others	☐ Individual: $104	☐ Institutional: $269

Call **888-378-2537** *or see mailing and pricing instructions below. Online subscriptions are available at www.interscience.wiley.com.*

Copy or detach page and send to:
**John Wiley & Sons, Journals Dept, 5th Floor
989 Market Street, San Francisco, CA 94103-1741**

Order Form can also be faxed to: 888-481-2665

Issue/Subscription Amount: $ _____	**SHIPPING CHARGES:**	
Shipping Amount: $ _____	SURFACE	Domestic Canadian
(for single issues only—subscription prices include shipping)	First Item	$5.00 $6.00
Total Amount: $ _____	Each Add'l Item	$3.00 $1.50

(No sales tax for U.S. subscriptions. Canadian residents, add GST for subscription orders. Individual rate subscriptions must be paid by personal check or credit card. Individual rate subscriptions may not be resold as library copies.)

☐ Payment enclosed (U.S. check or money order only. All payments must be in U.S. dollars.)

☐ VISA ☐ MC ☐ Amex # _____ Exp. Date _____

Card Holder Name _____ Card Issue # _____

Signature _____ Day Phone _____

☐ Bill Me (U.S. institutional orders only. Purchase order required.)

Purchase order # _____
                 Federal Tax ID13559302   GST 89102 8052

Name _____

Address _____

Phone _____ E-mail _____

JB7ND

NEW DIRECTIONS FOR TEACHING AND LEARNING IS NOW AVAILABLE ONLINE AT WILEY INTERSCIENCE

What is Wiley InterScience?

Wiley InterScience is the dynamic online content service from John Wiley & Sons delivering the full text of over 300 leading scientific, technical, medical, and professional journals, plus major reference works, the acclaimed Current Protocols laboratory manuals, and even the full text of select Wiley print books online.

What are some special features of Wiley InterScience?

Wiley Interscience Alerts is a service that delivers table of contents via e-mail for any journal available on Wiley InterScience as soon as a new issue is published online.

EarlyView is Wiley's exclusive service presenting individual articles online as soon as they are ready, even before the release of the compiled print issue. These articles are complete, peer-reviewed, and citable.

CrossRef is the innovative multi-publisher reference linking system enabling readers to move seamlessly from a reference in a journal article to the cited publication, typically located on a different server and published by a different publisher.

How can I access Wiley InterScience?

Visit http://www.interscience.wiley.com.

Guest Users can browse Wiley InterScience for unrestricted access to journal tables of contents and article abstracts, or use the powerful search engine.

Registered Users are provided with a *Personal Home Page* to store and manage customized alerts, searches, and links to favorite journals and articles. Additionally, Registered Users can view free online sample issues and preview selected material from major reference works.

Licensed Customers are entitled to access full-text journal articles in PDF, with select journals also offering full-text HTML.

How do I become an Authorized User?

Authorized Users are individuals authorized by a paying Customer to have access to the journals in Wiley InterScience. For example, a university that subscribes to Wiley journals is considered to be the Customer. Faculty, staff, and students authorized by the university to have access to those journals in Wiley InterScience are Authorized Users. Users should contact their library for information on which Wiley journals they have access to in Wiley InterScience.

UNITED STATES POSTAL SERVICE®

Statement of Ownership, Management, and Circulation
(All Periodicals Publications Except Requester Publications)

1. Publication Title	2. Publication Number	3. Filing Date
New Directions for Teaching and Learning	0 2 7 1 – 0 6 3 3	10/1/2007

4. Issue Frequency	5. Number of Issues Published Annually	6. Annual Subscription Price
Quarterly	4	$209

7. Complete Mailing Address of Known Office of Publication (Not printer) (Street, city, county, state, and ZIP+4®)

Wiley Subscriptions Services, Inc. at Jossey-Bass, 989 Market St., San Francisco, CA 94103

Contact Person: Joe Schuman
Telephone (Include area code): 415-782-3232

8. Complete Mailing Address of Headquarters or General Business Office of Publisher (Not printer)

Wiley Subscriptions Services, Inc., 111 River Street, Hoboken, NJ 07030

9. Full Names and Complete Mailing Addresses of Publisher, Editor, and Managing Editor (Do not leave blank)

Publisher (Name and complete mailing address)

Wiley Subscriptions Services, Inc., A Wiley Company at San Francisco, 989 Market St., San Francisco, CA 94103-1741

Editor (Name and complete mailing address)

Marilla D. Svinicki, Center for Teaching Effectiveness/University of Austin, Main Bldg., 2200 Austin, TX 78712-1111

Managing Editor (Name and complete mailing address)

None

10. Owner (Do not leave blank. If the publication is owned by a corporation, give the name and address of the corporation immediately followed by the names and addresses of all stockholders owning or holding 1 percent or more of the total amount of stock. If not owned by a corporation, give the names and addresses of the individual owners. If owned by a partnership or other unincorporated firm, give its name and address as well as those of each individual owner. If the publication is published by a nonprofit organization, give its name and address.)

Full Name	Complete Mailing Address
Wiley Subscriptions Services	111 River Street, Hoboken, NJ
(see attached list)	

11. Known Bondholders, Mortgagees, and Other Security Holders Owning or Holding 1 Percent or More of Total Amount of Bonds, Mortgages, or Other Securities. If none, check box ▶ ☑ None

Full Name	Complete Mailing Address

12. Tax Status (For completion by nonprofit organizations authorized to mail at nonprofit rates) (Check one)
The purpose, function, and nonprofit status of this organization and the exempt status for federal income tax purposes:
☐ Has Not Changed During Preceding 12 Months
☐ Has Changed During Preceding 12 Months (Publisher must submit explanation of change with this statement)

13. Publication Title	14. Issue Date for Circulation Data
New Directions for Teaching and Learning	Summer 2007

15. Extent and Nature of Circulation		Average No. Copies Each Issue During Preceding 12 Months	No. Copies of Single Issue Published Nearest to Filing Date
a. Total Number of Copies (Net press run)		1593	1356
b. Paid Circulation (By Mail and Outside the Mail)	(1) Mailed Outside-County Paid Subscriptions Stated on PS Form 3541(Include paid distribution above nominal rate, advertiser's proof copies, and exchange copies)	691	668
	(2) Mailed In-County Paid Subscriptions Stated on PS Form 3541 (Include paid distribution above nominal rate, advertiser's proof copies, and exchange copies)	0	0
	(3) Paid Distribution Outside the Mails Including Sales Through Dealers and Carriers, Street Vendors, Counter Sales, and Other Paid Distribution Outside USPS®	0	0
	(4) Paid Distribution by Other Classes of Mail Through the USPS (e.g. First-Class Mail®)	0	0
c. Total Paid Distribution (Sum of 15b (1), (2), (3), and (4))		691	668
d. Free or Nominal Rate Distribution (By Mail and Outside the Mail)	(1) Free or Nominal Rate Outside-County Copies (included on PS Form 3541	28	26
	(2) Free or Nominal Rate In-County Copies Included on PS Form 3541	0	0
	(3) Free or Nominal Rate Copies Mailed at Other Classes Through the USPS (e.g. First-Class Mail)	0	0
	(4) Free or Nominal Rate Distribution Outside the Mail (Carriers or other means)	0	0
e. Total Free or Nominal Rate Distribution (Sum of 15d (1), (2), (3) and (4)		28	26
f. Total Distribution (Sum of 15c and 15e) ▶		719	694
g. Copies not Distributed (See Instructions to Publishers #4 (page #3)) ▶		874	662
h. Total (Sum of 15f and g) ▶		1593	1356
i. Percent Paid (15c divided by 15f times 100) ▶		96%	96%

16. Publication of Statement of Ownership

☑ If the publication is a general publication, publication of this statement is required. Will be printed in the **WINTER 2007** issue of this publication.

☐ Publication not required

17. Signature and Title of Editor, Publisher, Business Manager, or Owner	Date
Susan E. Lewis, VP & Publisher - Periodicals *(signature)*	10/1/2007

I certify that all information furnished on this form is true and complete. I understand that anyone who furnishes false or misleading information on this form or who omits material or information requested on the form may be subject to criminal sanctions (including fines and imprisonment) and/or civil sanctions (including civil penalties)

42363952R00074

Made in the USA
Middletown, DE
09 April 2017